Medical Malpractice Legislation

Reforms in Civil Law Systems

Carlo Maria Masieri

Routledge
Taylor & Francis Group

LONDON AND NEW YORK

First published 2024
by Routledge
4 Park Square, Milton Park, Abingdon, Oxon OX14 4RN

and by Routledge
605 Third Avenue, New York, NY 10158

Routledge is an imprint of the Taylor & Francis Group, an informa business

© 2024 Carlo Maria Masieri

The right of Carlo Maria Masieri to be identified as author of this work has been asserted in accordance with sections 77 and 78 of the Copyright, Designs and Patents Act 1988.

British Library Cataloguing-in-Publication Data
A catalogue record for this book is available from the British Library

Library of Congress Cataloging-in-Publication Data
A catalog record for this book has been requested

ISBN: 978-1-032-57628-2 (hbk)
ISBN: 978-1-032-57629-9 (pbk)
ISBN: 978-1-003-44027-7 (ebk)

DOI: 10.4324/9781003440277

Typeset in Times New Roman
by Apex CoVantage, LLC

Contents

Abbreviations

ADSP	Actualité et dossier en santé publique
AJDA	L'Actualité juridique: Droit Administratif
AJLM	American Journal of Law and Medicine
Am J Comp L	American Journal of Comparative Law
Am J Forensic Med Pathol	The American Journal of Forensic Medicine and Pathology
Anaesth Crit Care Pain Med	Anaesthesia Critical Care & Pain Medicine
ANIA	Associazione Nazionale fra le Imprese Assicuratrici
Ann Fr Anesth Réanim	Annales françaises d'anesthésie et de reanimation
AOK	Allgemeine Ortskrankenkasse
Arch Intern Med	Archives of internal medicine
BGB	Bürgerliches Gesetzbuch
BGBl	Bundesgesetzblatt
BGH	Bundesgerichtshof
BMC Res Notes	BMC Research Notes
BMJ	British Medical Journal
Bull crim	Bulletin des arrêts de la chambre criminelle
C assur	Code des assurances
c c	Codice civile
C civ	Code civil
c p c	Codice di procedura civile
c p p	Codice di procedura penale
c p	Codice penale
C pén	Code pénal
C pr civ	Code de procédure civile
C pr pén	Code de procédure pénale
Cass civ	Corte di Cassazione – sezioni civili

Cass pen	Corte di Cassazione – sezioni penali
Cass	Cour de Cassation
CE	Conseil d'État
Clin Orthop Relat Res	Clinical Orthopaedics and Related Research
CNAMed	Commission nationale des accidents médicaux
Cogn Tech Work	Cognition, Technology & Work
Contr Impr Eur	Contratto e impresa. Europa
Contr Impr	Contratto e Impresa
Corte cost	Corte costituzionale
Cost	Costituzione
CPR	Civil Procedure Rules
CSP	Code de la santé publique
D	Recueil Dalloz
Danno e Resp	Danno e Responsabilità
Dir Pen Cont Riv Trim	Diritto penale contemporaneo Rivista Trimestrale
DMW	Deutsche Medizinische Wochenschrift
DP	Dalloz périodique
Dtsch Ärztebl	Deutsches Ärzteblatt
Empir Econ	Empirical Economics
Epidemiol Prev	Epidemiologia e Prevenzione
Fed R Evid	Federal Rules of Evidence
Foro It	Il Foro Italiano
GAMM	Groupe des assurances mutuelles médicales
GDV	Gesamtverband der Deutschen Versicherungswirtschaft
Geburtsh Frauenheilk	Geburtshilfe und Frauenheilkunde
GesR	GesundheitsRecht
GiurIt	Giurisprudenza Italiana
Giust Civ	Giustizia Civile
GU	Gazzetta Ufficiale della Repubblica Italiana
Gynäkologe	Der Gynäkologe
Health Econ	Health Economics
Int J Environ Res Public Health	International Journal of Environmental Research and Public Health
Int J Legal Med	International Journal of Legal Medicine
Inves Radiol	Investigative Radiology
IVASS	Istituto per la Vigilanza sulle Assicurazioni
J Law Med Ethics	Journal of Law, Medicine & Ethics

J Perinat Med	Journal of Perinatal Medicine
JAMA	Journal of the American Medical Association
JCPG	Juris Classeur Périodique Edition Générale
JETL	Journal of European Tort Law
JuS	Juristische Schulung
L Med & Health Care	Law, Medicine & Health Care
LCP	Law and Contemporary Problems
Lebon	Recueil des arrêts du Conseil d'État (Lebon)
MACSF	Mutuelle d'assurances du corps de santé français
MDK	Medizinische Dienst der Krankenversicherung
MDR	Monatsschrift für Deutsches Recht
Méd Mal Infect	Médecine et Maladies Infectieuses
MedR	Medizinrecht
Neurosurg Focus	Neurosurgical Focus
NJW	Neue Juristische Wochenschrift
Nuova Giur Civ Comm	La Nuova Giurisprudenza Civile Commentata
Ohio St LJ	Ohio State Law Journal
ONIAM	Office national d'indemnisation des accidents médicaux, des affections iatrogènes et des infections nosocomiales
ORM	Observatoire des risques médicaux
PN	Professional Negligence
Resp civ et assur	Responsabilité civile et assurances
Resp Civ Prev	Responsabilità Civile e Previdenza
Rev Intern Dr Comp	Revue internationale de droit comparé
Rh ÄBl	Rheinisches Ärzteblatt
Risques	Risques – Les cahiers de l'assurance
RiStBV	Richtlinien für das Strafverfahren und das Bußgeldverfahren
Riv Dir Civ	Rivista di Diritto Civile
Riv It Med Leg	Rivista italiana di medicina legale e del diritto in campo sanitario
RTDCiv	Revue trimestrielle de droit civil
RZPO	Reichszivilprozeßordnung
SGB	Sozialgesetzbuch
StGB	Strafgesetzbuch
StPO	Strafprozessordnung
UChLRev	University of Chicago Law Review

VersR	Versicherungsrecht
VW	Versicherungswirtschaft
ZEFQ	Zeitschrift für Evidenz, Fortbildung und Qualität im Gesundheitswesen
ZPO	Zivilprozessordnung

Introduction

Medical malpractice is an evergreen subject. Since the Code of Hammurabi,[1] lawmakers have passed countless laws addressing the potentially harmful effects of medical treatment.[2]

This issue cyclically rises to the top of the political agenda in many countries, being also related to the professional interests of the medical class – as well as lawyers. Medical malpractice law is further intertwined with more general health policy issues, on which the public opinion has focused for quite some time.

Legal scholars have exhibited a constant interest in this field of law, especially from a comparative perspective. Indeed, several contributions have been published on medical malpractice (both past[3] and recent),[4] continuously enriching the debate and the knowledge of this subject.

Scholarly contribution usually pertains to the reasons a set of rules should (or should not) be reformed. While such arguments may be ideologically based, quantitative analysis also plays a significant role. In the US, the social and political concern about medical malpractice that drove the reform

---

1 Robert F Harper (tr), *The Code of Hammurabi* (U of Chicago P 1904) 79, paras 218–20.
2 Arnaud Léger, Cécile Manaouil, Dominique Montpellier, Marie-Laure Moquet-Anger and Philippe Pierre, 'Responsabilité médicale et expertise: de la loi du Talion à la loi Kouchner' (2023) 2023 Médecine & Droit 7, 7–9.
3 Ewoud Hondius (ed), *The Development of Medical Liability* (CUP 2010); Bernhard E Koch (ed), *Medical Liability in Europe: A Comparison of Selected Jurisdictions* (De Gruyter 2011); Ken Oliphant and Richard W Wright (eds), *Medical Malpractice and Compensation in Global Perspective* (De Gruyter 2013).
4 Dobrochna Bach-Golecka, 'Compensation Schemes and Extra-Judicial Solutions in Case of Medical Malpractice: A Commentary on Contemporary Arrangements', in Katharina Boele-Woelki, Diego P Fernández Arroyo and Alexandre Senegacnik (eds), *General Reports of the XXth General Congress of the International Academy of Comparative Law* (Springer 2020); Anthony J Sebok, 'Recovery for Physical Harm: The Case of Medical Malpractice', in Mauro Bussani, Anthony J Sebok and Marta Infantino (eds), *Common Law and Civil Law Perspectives on Tort Law* (OUP 2022).

DOI: 10.4324/9781003440277-1

movement since the mid-1970s was backed by several quantitative studies,[5] often suggesting the existence of medical malpractice crises. Hence, scholars delved into the extent of such crises.

The same approach can also be found in some comparative works, which examine other Common Law systems, including England.[6] There, at the end of the XX century, legal innovations in this field were primarily adopted in the ambit of the reform of civil procedure rules,[7] albeit there was additionally an administrative reorganisation on the defendants' side that established a unified claims management system for the National Healthcare System (NHS)[8] and granted indemnity to doctors employed by its hospitals.[9] Finally, after considerable study,[10] the NHS Redress Act of 2006[11] authorised the Secretary of State to adopt a compensation scheme for medical injuries that occurred in NHS hospitals; however, this scheme has yet to be adopted. Nonetheless, the debate on a potential NHS litigation reform is still ongoing.[12]

In contrast, several Civil Law countries have already reformed their medical malpractice laws. For instance, France underwent reforms in 2002.[13]

---

5 Paul C Weiler, *Medical Malpractice on Trial* (Harvard UP 1991) 3, 165–68, 187–88.
6 Chris Ham, Robert Dingwall, Paul Fenn and Don Harris, *Medical Negligence: Compensation and Accountability* (King's Fund Institute 1988); Frances H Miller, 'Medical Malpractice Litigation: Do the British Have a Better Remedy?' (1986) 11 AJLM 433; Patricia M Danzon, 'The Crisis in Medical Malpractice: A Comparison of Trends in the United States, Canada, the United Kingdom and Australia' (1990) 18 L Med & Health Care 48; Donald N Dewees, Michael J Trebilcock and Peter C Coyte, 'The Medical Malpractice Crisis: A Comparative Empirical Perspective' (1991) 54 LCP 217; Kay Wheat, 'Is There a Medical Malpractice Crisis in the UK?' (2005) J Law Med Ethics 444.
7 Harry Woolf, *Access to Justice: To the Lord Chancellor on the Civil Justice System in England and Wales* (H.M. Stationery Office 1996); Civil Procedure Rules 1998; *Pre-Action Protocol for the Resolution of Clinical Disputes.*
8 National Health Service and Community Care Act 1990 s 1; National Health Service (Clinical Negligence Scheme) Regulations 1996, SI 1996/251.
9 Department of Health, *Claims of Medical Negligence against N.H.S. Hospital and Community Doctors and Dentists,* HC (89) 34; Department of Health, *NHS Indemnity: Arrangements for Clinical Negligence Claims in the NHS,* HSG 96/48.
10 Liam Donaldson, *Making Amends: A Consultation Paper Setting Out Proposals for Reforming the Approach to Clinical Negligence in the NHS – A Report by the Chief Medical Officer* (Department of Health Publications 2003).
11 From a critical perspective, see Anne-Maree Farrell and Sarah Devaney, 'Making Amends or Making Things Worse? Clinical Negligence Reform and Patient Redress in England' (2007) 27 LS 630.
12 Health and Social Care Committee, *NHS Litigation Reform: Thirteenth Report of Session 2021–22* (House of Commons 2022) <https://publications.parliament.uk/pa/cm5802/cmselect/cmhealth/740/report.html#heading-5> accessed 28 June 2023.
13 *Loi n°2002-303 du 4 mars 2002 relative aux droits des malades et à la qualité du système de santé,* the so-called *loi Kouchner; loi n°2002-1577 du 30 décembre 2002 relative à la responsabilité civile médicale,* the so-called *loi About.*

Almost at the same time, Germany modified its statute of limitations[14] and certain aspects of damages;[15] a specific medical malpractice act was passed around 10 years later.[16] In 2012, Italy enacted its first designated medical malpractice law,[17] and another one in 2017.[18]

Thus, it is first interesting to assess whether any medical malpractice crises have been identified in these systems, and, second, how these have been faced through the passing of new statutes on the Continent.

Accordingly, the first chapter explores the idea of medical malpractice crisis and its relationship with the insurance market, also considering the reflections of American scholars. It then reconstructs the French, German and Italian legal frameworks, as well as their insurance and litigation contexts, reviewing and commenting on the quantitative evidence that was collected before the reforms.

The second chapter briefly summarises the debate on medical malpractice reforms in France, Germany and Italy. It then analyses the statutes that have been passed, distinguishing between reforms that consolidate case law and reforms that introduce innovative solutions, sometimes repealing doctrines developed by the courts. In particular, the chapter examines in a comparative perspective the different options adopted in these Civil Law countries with regard to the rules on liability, burden of proof, statute of limitations and damages. Moreover, the chapter examines the reforms of insurance, procedural and evidence law, to the extent they affect medical malpractice cases.

The third chapter reviews and analyses the current available data related to medical malpractice litigation and insurance after the reforms adopted in France, Germany and Italy, in order to find out evidence of their effectiveness and efficiency. It also highlights some aspects of medical malpractice law that still belong to the domain of the judiciary. It finally points out which problems may be addressed by the legislatures and what further data should be collected in the future.

---

14 By passing the *Gesetz zur Modernisierung des Schuldrechts vom 26. November 2001 (BGBl I S 3138)*, the so-called *Schuldrechtsmodernisierungsgesetz*.

15 *Zweites Gesetz zur Änderung schadensersatzrechtlicher Vorschriften vom 19. Juli 2002 (BGBl I S 2674)*, the so-called *Zweites Schadensersatzrechtsänderungsgesetz*.

16 *Gesetz zur Verbesserung der Rechte von Patientinnen und Patienten vom 20. Februar 2013 (BGBl I S 277)*, the so-called *Patientenrechtegesetz*.

17 *Decreto legge 13 settembre 2012, n 158 conv con modif in legge 8 novembre 2012, n 189*, the so-called *decreto Balduzzi*.

18 *Legge 8 marzo 2017, n 24*, the so-called *legge Gelli-Bianco*.

1 Medical Malpractice Before Reforms

Was There Any Crisis?

What Crisis?

The American scholarly literature on medical malpractice crises frequently refers to higher liability insurance premiums[1] and companies leaving the market.[2] In other words, the increase of insurance premiums for practitioners has been considered a major indicator of a crisis, as it is likely attributable to increasing medical malpractice litigation and huge damages awards,[3] which are related to the special features of the US procedural model.[4]

This approach has been criticised.[5] To begin with, economic arguments point out that other factors are capable of independently causing premiums to soar. For instance, reinsurance costs (which depended in turn on extreme events that may have been completely unrelated to medical malpractice),[6] general insurance market conditions and errors in companies' predictions[7] are cited.

Further criticisms come from another perspective more focused on the aims of tort law, and especially of medical malpractice. Some scholars note that if this field of law aims to award adequate compensation to the victims of medical accidents, then a crisis could be represented by the fact that too few meritorious cases generate claims.[8] In the US, this is evidenced by data from a Californian hospital records study and closed insurance claims;[9] subsequently, a discrepancy between the high number of medical errors and the fewer litigated cases

---

1 Paul C Weiler, *Medical Malpractice on Trial* (Harvard UP 1991) 3, 165–68, 187–88, 2, 8–11.
2 ibid 27.
3 ibid 2–3.
4 ibid 8–16, 48–49.
5 Frank A Sloan and Lindsey M Chepke, *Medical Malpractice* (MIT Press 2008) vii, 5–6, 9–11.
6 ibid 255.
7 Tom Baker, *The Medical Malpractice Myth* (Chicago UP 2005) 51–58.
8 Richard L Abel, 'Real Tort Crisis – Too Few Claims' (1987) 48 Ohio St LJ 443, 447; Baker (n 7) 2–3, 6–8, 68–70.
9 California Medical Association, *Medical Insurance Feasibility Study* (Sutter Publications 1977); Patricia Danzon, *Medical Malpractice: Theory, Evidence, and Public Policy* (Harvard UP 1985).

DOI: 10.4324/9781003440277-2

emerged from a very famous multidisciplinary hospital records study in the State of New York,[10] which was confirmed by further research.[11]

At the same time, insurance may be considered a tool for the proper functioning of the tort system, improving the efficacy of how compensation is awarded to victims. Accordingly, information from the insurance market should not be neglected.

That is why we will look at data collected by several studies concerning the Civil Law systems, on the availability and costs of medical malpractice liability insurance, on the costs of that liability, as well as on adverse events.

Defensive medicine and its costs,[12] which are difficult to track,[13] should also be investigated, as they are often considered a consequence of medical malpractice crisis.

A Law Beyond Statutes

A brief overview of medical malpractice law in Civil Law systems before the age of reforms might be useful, especially for those who are unfamiliar with these systems. This field is indeed a paradigm of the interactions between different legal formants.[14]

Interestingly, at the end of the XX century, a significant portion of medical malpractice law in these countries was contained in court decisions rather than statute law.

France

In the French system, the general rules on tort[15] and on breach of obligation[16] have been enshrined in the *Code civil* since its promulgation in 1804. However, a specific institutional feature of France must be pointed out: there

---

10 Harvard Medical Practice Study Group, *Patients, Doctors, and Lawyers: Medical Injury, Malpractice Litigation and Patient Compensation in New York* (President and Fellows of Harvard College 1990).

11 Baker (n 7) 30–33.

12 Weiler (n 1) 10.

13 Baker (n 7) 118ff.

14 Rodolfo Sacco, 'Legal Formants: A Dynamic Approach to Comparative Law' (1991) 39 Am J Comp L 1, 22–24.

15 C civ, art 1382: 'Tout fait quelconque de l'homme, qui cause à autrui un dommage, oblige celui par la faute duquel il est arrivé à le réparer'.
   C civ, art 1383: 'Chacun est responsable du dommage qu'il a causé non seulement par son fait, mais encore par sa négligence ou par son imprudence'.

16 C civ, art 1147: 'Le débiteur est condamné, s'il y a lieu, au paiement de dommages et intérêts, soit à raison de l'inexécution de l'obligation, soit à raison du retard dans l'exécution, toutes les fois qu'il ne justifie pas que l'inexécution provient d'une cause étrangère qui ne peut lui être imputée, encore qu'il n'y ait aucune mauvaise foi de sa part'.

is a long-standing division between the private and public sectors, which is primarily reflected in the existence of separate jurisdictions.

If medical treatment is performed in a state-owned facility,[17] an administrative tribunal has jurisdiction[18] in the event a damages case is brought against a state hospital. In the past, this could only be liable for gross negligence,[19] and the limitation period was four years '*à partir du premier jour de l'année suivant celle au cours de laquelle les droits ont été acquis*' ('from the first day of the year following the year in which the entitlements arose');[20] that is, from the date the harm occurred (not the date of treatment) in permanent bodily injury cases.[21]

The clinicians employed by those hospitals could be deemed individually liable in tort by a civil or a criminal court, bearing in mind that the victim can seek damages also in criminal trials. However, damages could only be awarded if a doctor's conduct, due to its nature or its special grossness, materially deviated from his public service duties,[22] eg refusing[23] or otherwise omitting[24] to perform an urgent treatment despite an express request. In fact, this has been found in a very few cases.

Damages cases against private hospitals and their clinicians are heard by the civil courts, without prejudice to the aggrieved party's right to damages in criminal proceedings – as will be discussed later.

Since the high-profile *arrête Mercier* case,[25] independent practitioners have been considered liable to their patients in contract. On this point, it is worth mentioning another special feature of French law: actions in tort and those in contract are not concurrent,[26] and, as it has been observed,[27] in the past the choice between them bore significance mostly with regard to the statute of limitations. On this topic, the decisions of the courts intertwined with several reforms.

17 Emmanuel Terrier and Jean Penneau, 'Médecine: réparation des conséquences des risques sanitaires', *Répertoire de droit civil Dalloz* (Octobre 2020) (actualisation: Mars 2023) paras 274–75 <www-dalloz-fr> accessed 2 May 2023; Caroline Grossholz, 'Hôpitaux: régimes de responsabilité et de solidarité', *Répertoire de la responsabilité de la puissance publique Dalloz* (Février 2018) (actualisation: Février 2023) paras 6–16 <www-dalloz-fr> accessed 2 May 2023.

18 On the distinction between administrative tribunals and civil courts in France, see Antonio Gambaro, 'Francia', *Digesto delle discipline privatistiche: Sezione civile*, vol 8 (1992) para 7.

19 CE 8 novembre 1935, *Dame Vion, épouse Loiseau et Dame Philipponeau*, Lebon 1019.

20 *Loi n° 68–1250 du 31 décembre 1968*, art 1; Grossholz (n 17) para 36.

21 André Lefeuvre, 'De la prescription décennale en matière de responsabilité médicale' (2003) AJDA 270.

22 Grossholz (n 17) paras 153–55; Jean-Marie Auby, 'La responsabilité médicale en France (aspects de droit public)' (1976) 28 Rev Intern Dr Comp 511, 514–15; Marcel-René Tercinet, 'Principes généraux de la responsabilité médicale sur le plan administratif' (1998) 28 Méd Mal Infect 41, 42.

23 CE 4 juillet 1990, *Société d'assurances 'Le Sou Médical' c/ Centre hospitalier général de Gap*, req no 63930, Lebon T 972.

24 Crim 2 avril 1991, no 90–87.579, Bull crim no 140.

25 Civ 20 mai 1936, DP 1936. 1. 88, concl Matter, rapp Josserand, note EP.

26 Pier Giuseppe Monateri, 'Cumulo di azioni', *Digesto delle discipline privatistiche: Sezione civile*, vol 3 (1989) para 2.

27 Claudia Amodio, 'La responsabilità medica nell'esperienza francese: profili comparatistici' (2002) Contr Impr Eur 528, 560.

While once tort actions and contract-based lawsuits were both time-barred in 30 years, the latter was not subject to the French principle of the unity of civil and criminal limitation periods, which affected only tort cases.[28] This was the situation until 1980, when the principle was abandoned by the legislature.[29]

In 1985, with *loi n°85–677*, tort actions against private facilities became subject to a new 10-year time limit running '*à compter de la manifestation du dommage ou de son aggravation*' ('from the appearance of the injury or its worsening'),[30] distinguishing them from contract-based lawsuits; although the courts calculated the limitation period from the time of consolidation of bodily injuries, which was potentially subsequent to the starting point established under the new law (ie when injury appears).[31] Conversely, as stated earlier, actions against state hospitals were time-barred in just four years.

In any event, as will be illustrated in the next chapter, French law on limitation periods has been reformed several times since the 1980s.

Regarding the difference between breach of contractual obligations and tortious negligence, the French courts distinguished between *obligations de résultat* and *obligations de moyens*, which in this country is linked to the scholarly works of Demogue.[32] However, the origins of this doctrine are uncertain, as it appears to be a common trait in Civil Law systems, having been adopted also in Italy and in Germany.[33]

Nevertheless, it must be observed that use of the *obligation de moyens* in French medical malpractice cases is coeval with the introduction of contractual liability: both date back to *arrête Mercier*.[34] Indeed, this way, contract-based medical malpractice lawsuits enjoyed *de facto* a longer limitation period, but at the same time placed the same burden of proof on claimants as required for negligence cases, which characterised tort actions.

Regarding causation, the distinction between tort and contract in France is irrelevant, as in both cases the claimant must demonstrate the existence of a causal link between the defendant's conduct and the harm.[35] Furthermore, while the causal link must be ascertained with certainty, presumptions make it possible to overcome this formality, and loss of chance is broadly compensated in the case law.[36]

---

28 Daniel Bert, 'Feu l'arrêt Mercier!' (2010) D 1801.

29 *Loi n°80–1042 du 23 décembre 1980.*

30 *Loi n°85–677 du 5 juillet 1985*, art 38 introduced a 10-year limitation period for tort actions into C civ, art 2270–1.

31 Patrice Jourdain, 'Prescription de l'action en responsabilité extra-contractuelle: en cas de dommage corporel, le délai de la prescription court du jour de la consolidation' (2000) RTDCiv 851.

32 René Demogue, *Traité des obligations en general V* (Librairie Arthur Rousseau 1925) nos 1237ff.

33 Valeria De Lorenzi, 'Obbligazioni di mezzi e obbligazioni di risultato', *Digesto delle discipline privatistiche: Sezione civile*, vol 12 (1995) paras 1–2 and fns 1 and 16.

34 See n 25.

35 Terrier and Peannau (n 17) paras 373, 384ff.

36 Simon Taylor, *Medical Accident Liability and Redress in English and French Law* (CUP 2015) 42–46.

Like in other Western countries, until the 1950s, suits against healthcare providers were a rarity in France; the rise of medical malpractice litigation and the activism of the French judiciary came later.[37] Therefore, even though this Civil Law system appears very different from Common Law systems from a structural perspective, their respective social behaviour and historical paths are quite similar.

The contribution of the French judiciary became particularly relevant in the years immediately preceding the age of reforms. As it has been observed,[38] towards the end of the XX century, courts increasingly recognised strict liability in medical malpractice law. This was the case, for instance, when a bacterial infection occurred in a private hospital.[39]

For public hospitals, strict liability was introduced for so-called *aléa thérapeutique* cases (ie when medical treatments cause extremely severe injuries unrelated to the patient's initial condition or to its foreseeable development)[40] while the gross fault requirement was abandoned, meaning public hospitals could be liable for all degrees of negligence.[41]

During this period, private healthcare facilities (not employee doctors) were contractually liable to patients; employee clinicians of private hospitals were individually responsible towards the patients[42] only in cases of intentional infliction of harm or when the conduct constituted a criminal offense.[43]

Germany

In Germany, since 1900, the BGB has been the point of reference for the general rules on tort,[44] and its provisions on *Dienstvertrag*[45] (literally, 'the service

---

37 Jean Penneau, *La responsabilité médicale* (Sirey 1977) 2.

38 Sophie Gromb, 'Responsabilité médicale: va-t-on indemniser l'accident mèdical?' (1996) 16 Médecine & Droit 12, 14; Taylor (n 36) 25.

39 Cass 1re civ 29 juin 1999, JCP G 1999 II, 10138, rapp P Sargos.

40 CE 4 avril 1993, *Bianchi*, JCP G 1993 II, 22061, note J Moreau; to the contrary, this was rejected by civil courts, see Cass 1re civ 8 novembre 2000, RTDCiv 2001, 154, obs. J. Mestre.

41 CE 10 avril 1992, *Épx V*, Lebon 171.

42 Cass 1re civ 4 juin 1991, JCP G 1991 II, 21730, note J Savatier; Cass 1re civ 9 novembre 2004, D 2005, 253.

43 Terrier and Penneau (n 17) para 319.

44 § 823 BGB: '(1) Wer vorsätzlich oder fahrlässig das Leben, den Körper, die Gesundheit, die Freiheit, das Eigentum oder ein sonstiges Recht eines anderen widerrechtlich verletzt, ist dem anderen zum Ersatze des daraus entstehenden Schadens verpflichtet.

(2) ¹Die gleiche Verpflichtung trifft denjenigen, welcher gegen ein den Schutz eines anderen bezweckendes Gesetz verstößt. ²Ist nach dem Inhalte des Gesetzes ein Verstoß gegen dieses auch ohne Verschulden möglich, so tritt die Ersatzpflicht nur im Falle des Verschuldens ein'.

45 § 611 BGB: '(1) Durch den Dienstvertrag wird derjenige, welcher Dienste zusagt, zur Leistung der versprochenen Dienste, der andere Teil zur Gewährung der vereinbarten Vergütung verpflichtet.

(2) Gegenstand des Dienstvertrags können Dienste jeder Art sein'.

contract') made it possible to overcome much of the prior doctrinal debate on the legal relationship between patients and independent practitioners.[46]

Despite codification, a contract law analysis of medical malpractice remained challenging. The open issues were primarily attributable to the special features of German healthcare, a model established by Chancellor Otto von Bismarck, with mandatory health insurance covering most of the population and paying for outpatient services rendered mostly by independent practitioners, as well as inpatient treatments performed in public and private hospitals.[47]

Yet, intromitting insurance funds in the patient-healthcare provider relationship did not engender excessive complications: the issue was resolved by the German judiciary in just a few years. Applying § 328 BGB,[48] courts found that the insured were beneficiaries of third-party rights arising from the contracts between the insurance funds and the healthcare providers. Accordingly, in the event of malpractice, insured patients could sue hospitals and clinicians in contract.[49] And later on, a contractual relationship was recognised to exist between the patient and the admitting hospital and/or the clinician (depending on the circumstances) regardless of how the medical services are paid.[50]

As concerns redress, just as in other countries, compensation for harm caused by medical treatments is an issue also in Germany.

Unlike in France, German civil courts have jurisdiction over medical malpractice cases, independent of the private or public nature of the defendant.[51] And, as will be discussed later, in Germany, criminal liability and criminal courts seem to play a rather secondary role.

Furthermore, in the past, there were considerable differences between actions in tort and actions in contract. For instance, contract claims were subject

---

46 Colm P McGrath, *The Development of Medical Liability in Germany, 1800–1945* (Vittorio Klostermann 2019) 139–49.

47 Frantz M Petry, 'Medical Liability in Germany', in Bernhard E Koch (ed), *Medical Liability in Europe: A Comparison of Selected Jurisdictions* (De Gruyter 2011) 233–37; Marc S Stauch, 'Medical Malpractice and Compensation in Germany', in Ken Oliphant and Richard W Wright (eds), *Medical Malpractice and Compensation in Global Perspective* (De Gruyter 2013) 179–81.

48 § 328 BGB: '(1) Durch Vertrag kann eine Leistung an einen Dritten mit der Wirkung bedungen werden, daß der Dritte unmittelbar das Recht erwirbt, die Leistung zu fordern.

(2) In Ermangelung einer besonderen Bestimmung ist aus den Umständen, insbesondere aus dem Zwecke des Vertrags, zu entnehmen, ob der Dritte das Recht erwerben, ob das Recht des Dritten sofort oder nur unter gewissen Voraussetzungen entstehen und ob den Vertragschließenden die Befugnis vorbehalten sein soll, das Recht des Dritten ohne dessen Zustimmung aufzuheben oder zu ändern'.

49 McGrath (n 46) 150–52.

50 Petry (n 47) 238–39, 256–61; Stauch (n 47) 184.

51 Petry (n 47) 266.

to a general 30-year limitation period[52] (commencing from the moment the right became actionable),[53] whereas tort suits were time-barred in three years from the moment the patient became aware of the harm and of the presumed tortfeasor, and, irrespective of such knowledge, after 30 years from the commission of the tortious act.[54] This long-stop period seems to fit well with so-called latent harms or long-tail claims (ie cases in which there is an extensive lag between the tortfeasor's conduct and the perception of its harmful effects by the victim), many of which occur in the medical field. As such, the German Civil Code attempted to balance the principle of discoverability and the general value of legal certainty; however, scholars suggested adopting even shorter long-stop periods.[55] It is also noteworthy that the absence of a maximum period for bringing claims clashes with the actuarial needs of the insurance industry, which is in turn essential to effectively compensate the victim.

Another important difference between contractual and tortious liability under former German law was that damages for pain and suffering were available only in tort suits;[56] however, the courts allowed concurrent actions in tort and in contract,[57] thus minimizing this difference.

Similarly to what happened with the *obligation de moyens* in France, the *Dienstvertrag* required German patients bear the same burden of proof as in tortious negligence cases.[58] And, like in the French experience, the German

---

52 § 195 BGB (*1. Januar 1900–1. Januar 2002*): 'Die regelmäßige Verjährungsfrist beträgt dreißig Jahre'.

53 § 198 BGB (*1. Januar 1900–1. Januar 2002*): '(1) Die Verjährung beginnt mit der Entstehung des Anspruchs. (2) Geht der Anspruch auf ein Unterlassen, so beginnt die Verjährung mit der Zuwiderhandlung'.

54 § 852 BGB (*1. Januar 1900–1. Januar 1978*): '(1) Der Anspruch auf Ersatz des aus einer unerlaubten Handlung entstandenen Schadens verjährt in drei Jahren von dem Zeitpunkt an, in welchem der Verletzte von dem Schaden und der Person des Ersatzpflichtigen Kenntnis erlangt, ohne Rücksicht auf diese Kenntnis in dreißig Jahren von der Begehung der Handlung an.

   (2) Hat der Ersatzpflichtige durch die unerlaubte Handlung auf Kosten des Verletzten etwas erlangt, so ist er auch nach der Vollendung der Verjährung zur Herausgabe nach den Vorschriften über die Herausgabe einer ungerechtfertigten Bereicherung verpflichtet'.

55 Reinhard Zimmermann, *Comparative Foundations of a European Law of Set-Off and Prescription* (CUP 2002) 99ff.

56 § 253 BGB: 'Wegen eines Schadens, der nicht Vermögensschaden ist, kann Entschädigung in Geld nur in den durch das Gesetz bestimmten Fällen gefordert werden'.

   § 847(1) BGB: '¹Im Falle der Verletzung des Körpers oder der Gesundheit sowie im Falle der Freiheitsentziehung kann der Verletzte auch wegen des Schadens, der nicht Vermögensschaden ist, eine billige Entschädigung in Geld verlangen. ²Der Anspruch ist nicht übertragbar und geht nicht auf die Erben über, es sei denn, daß er durch Vertrag anerkannt oder daß er rechtshängig geworden ist'.

57 BGH 20.09.1988 – VI ZR 37/88, NJW 1989, 767.

58 Stauch (n 47) 185, 189.

judiciary shifted this burden in some cases – eg, when the harm was caused by defective medical equipment[59] or infections.[60]

Whether acting in tort or in contract, claimants were further required to establish causation,[61] with some exceptions developed by the German courts.[62]

Italy

In Italy, the difficulties of framing medical malpractice law according to a tort or traditional contract law analysis have resulted in this area of law being defined as a subsystem of civil liability,[63] rich of sectorial solutions advanced by the judiciary.

In addition to the general rules of tort,[64] the *Codice civile* of 1942 offered some specific contract law provisions[65] that appeared applicable to the professional activity of doctors and their liability. However, since the institution in 1978 of the *Servizio sanitario nazionale*[66] (the Italian health service), public facilities – with doctors as employees – are responsible for performing the majority of medical activities. Initially, the absence of a direct contractual relationship between clinicians and patients induced the Italian courts to allow claimants to bring only tort claims against these employed clinicians, whereas hospitals could be sued for breach of contract.[67]

After a period of uncertainty, the civil and criminal courts (instead of the administrative tribunals) had jurisdiction over medical malpractice cases, with the criminal courts gaining particular importance in this country.

---

59 BGH 11.10.1977 – VI ZR 110/75, NJW 1978, 584.

60 BGH 03.11.1981 – VI ZR 119/80, NJW 1982, 699.

61 BGH 17.12.1968 – VI ZR 212/67, NJW 1969, 553.

62 BGH 26.02.1991 – VI ZR 344/89, NJW 1991, 1540.

63 Raffaella De Matteis, *La responsabilità medica: Un sottosistema della responsabilità civile* (Cedam 1995); Cass civ sez III 16 ottobre 2007 n 21619, in DeJure <https://dejure.it> accessed 11 May 2023.

64 Art 2043 c c – Risarcimento per fatto illecito: 'Qualunque fatto doloso o colposo, che cagiona ad altri un danno ingiusto, obbliga colui che ha commesso il fatto a risarcire il danno'.

65 Art 2230 c c – Prestazione d'opera intellettuale: '[I]. Il contratto che ha per oggetto una prestazione d'opera intellettuale è regolato dalle norme seguenti e, in quanto compatibili con queste e con la natura del rapporto, dalle disposizioni del capo precedente.

[II]. Sono salve le disposizioni delle leggi speciali'.

Art. 2236 c c – Responsabilità del prestatore d'opera: 'Se la prestazione implica la soluzione di problemi tecnici di speciale difficoltà, il prestatore d'opera non risponde dei danni, se non in caso di dolo o di colpa grave'.

66 Francesco Taroni, *Health and Healthcare Policy in Italy since 1861: A Comparative Approach* (Palgrave Macmillan 2021) 165ff; Alessandra Pioggia, *Diritto sanitario e dei servizi sociali* (Giappichelli 2014) 77–78.

67 Cass civ sez III 24 marzo 1979 n 1716, in Foro It 1980 I, 1115; Cass civ sez III 26 marzo 1990 n 2428, in Giur It 1991 I, 600; Cass civ sez III 13 marzo 1998 n 2750, in Foro It 1998 I, 3521.

Tort suits are time-barred in five years; if a conduct constitutes a criminal offence and a longer limitation period is established for the offence, this longer period also applies to the civil action for damages,[68] whereas contract-based suits are subject to the ordinary time limit of 10 years.[69] However, according to case law, these periods start to run only when the victim perceives or may reasonably perceive that the harm has been caused by another's intentional or negligent conduct. And unlike German law, there is no counterbalancing provision, such as a long-stop period.[70]

Regarding the fault requirement, the judiciary broadly applied the *obbligazione di mezzi* doctrine,[71] so that the patients bore the same burden of proving negligence in both contract and tort actions. For similar purposes, judges extended the application of art 2236 c c, which exempts contractual liability when negligence is not gross and related to special technical difficulties, even in the absence of a contractual relationship.[72] The aforementioned article codifies the ideas of the French scholar Demogue. However, compared to Italy, the same approach has been more widely followed in France, even without a specific statutory provision.

At the same time, where routine treatments (generally executed with minimal risk to the patient) resulted in harm, the Italian courts facilitated the claimants through rebuttable presumptions.[73]

At the end of the XX century, embracing the scholar-made doctrine of *contatto sociale qualificato*,[74] the *Corte di cassazione* (Italy's highest civil and

---

68 Art 2947 c c – Prescrizione del diritto al risarcimento del danno: '[I]. Il diritto al risarcimento del danno derivante da fatto illecito si prescrive in cinque anni dal giorno in cui il fatto si è verificato. (. . .)
    [III.] In ogni caso, se il fatto è considerato dalla legge come reato e per il reato è stabilita una prescrizione più lunga, questa si applica anche all'azione civile. Tuttavia, se il reato è estinto per causa diversa dalla prescrizione o è intervenuta sentenza irrevocabile nel giudizio penale, il diritto al risarcimento del danno si prescrive nei termini indicati dai primi due commi, con decorrenza dalla data di estinzione del reato o dalla data in cui la sentenza è divenuta irrevocabile'.

69 Art 2946 c c – Prescrizione ordinaria: 'Salvi i casi in cui la legge dispone diversamente, i diritti si estinguono per prescrizione con il decorso di dieci anni'.

70 Mauro Tescaro, 'L'evoluzione del diritto della prescrizione: termini, decorrenze e cause di estensione' (2023) Riv Dir Civ 69, 82–83.

71 Cass civ sez un 9 marzo 1965, in Foro It 1965 I, 1040; Cass civ sez III 25 novembre 1994 n 10014, in Foro It 1995 I, 2913; some exceptions were made, in which an obligation of result was acknowledged, eg in cosmetic surgery, Cass civ sez III 25 novembre 1994 n 10014, in Foro It 1995 I, 2913.

72 Cass civ sez un 6 maggio 1971 n 1282, in Foro It 1971 I, 1475.

73 Cass civ sez III 21 dicembre 1978 n 6141, in Foro It 1979 I, 8.

74 Carlo Castronovo, 'L'obbligazione senza prestazione ai confini tra contratto e torto', in *Le ragioni del diritto: Scritti in onore di Luigi Mengoni I* (Giuffrè 1995) 147ff.

criminal court) held that – even in the absence of a proper contractual agreement – doctors employed by the hospitals could be held liable in contract.[75]

Subsequently, the same court changed the rules on the burden of proof for contractual liability,[76] requiring the patient to merely demonstrate the existence of an obligation and to allege that such obligation had been breached by the defendant.[77] Regarding the substance of the obligation, the healthcare provider is only required to perform the necessary or agreed medical treatment, without worsening the condition (albeit this standard is somewhat unclear), excluding any guarantee of recovery.

Art 2236 c c fell into disuse,[78] and the *Cassazione* also abandoned the *obbligazione di mezzi* doctrine,[79] specifying that the alleged breach should be abstractly capable of causing the harm, and that the harm had to be proved by the claimant.[80]

Scholars sharply pointed out that Italian medical malpractice thus became a sort of strict liability field.[81]

The Role of Medical Experts

It is noteworthy to recall a special feature of Civil Law systems: in these countries, the use of court-appointed expert witnesses is a practice dating back several years.[82] The following paragraphs continue to focus on the pre-reform era.

---

75 Cass civ sez III 22 aprile 1999 n 589, in Foro It 1999 I, 3331.

76 Initially, outside the medical malpractice field, Cass civ sez un 30 novembre 2001 n 13533, in Foro It 2002 I, 769.

77 Cass civ sez III 28 maggio 2004 n 10297, in Foro It 2005 I, 2479.

78 Giovanna Visintini, *Trattato breve della responsabilità civile* (Cedam 2005) 297.

79 Firstly, with regard to the liability of engineers, Cass civ sez un 28 luglio 2005 n 15781, in Nuova Giur Civ Comm 2006 I, 828.

80 Cass civ sez III 13 aprile 2007 n 8826, in Resp Civ Prev 2007, 1824; Cass civ sez un 11 gennaio 2008 n 577, in Resp Civ Prev 2008, 849; Cass civ sez III 18 settembre 2009 n 20101 in DeJure <https://dejure.it> accessed 12 May 2023.

81 Antonio Gambaro, 'Nuovi spunti in tema di responsabilità sanitaria nella prospettiva comparatistica', in *La responsabilità in materia sanitaria. Atti del Convegno nazionale tenuto a Bologna il 16 dicembre e a Ravenna il 17 dicembre 1983* (Giuffrè 1984), 38–39; Giulio Ponzanelli, 'Medical malpractice: la legge Bianco Gelli' (2017) Contr Impr 356, 357.

82 In the US, despite there being some rules (eg Fed R Evid 706), they are unused, especially in medical malpractice cases, see Carlo M Masieri, *Linee guida e responsabilità civile del medico. Dall'esperienza americana alla legge Gelli-Bianco* (Giuffrè Francis Lefebvre 2019) 74–75, 95–96; in England, since 1999, CPR 35.7 has allowed the appointment of a single joint expert, albeit its application in medical negligence cases has proven difficult, see Déirdre Dwyer, 'The Role of the Expert under CPR Pt 35', in Déirdre Dwyer (ed), *The Civil Procedure Rules Ten Years On* (OUP 2009) 317–19.

France

In France, the Code of Civil Procedure of 1806 encouraged the parties to agree on a board of three experts; absent an agreement, the court could appoint the board.[83] Specific reforms of 1944[84] and 1973,[85] as well as the Code of 1975,[86] indicated a preference for a single court-appointed expert witness. Judges are not bound by the opinion of their experts;[87] however, their testimony is central to any finding of negligence and causation.[88] *Expertise officieuse* (ie expert witness testimonies for the parties) have been also admitted, and judges can base their decisions on these rather on their own experts' opinions.[89]

The *référé* (ie a pre-trial order)[90] may direct an investigation, appoint an expert or, if the existence of liability is not seriously questionable, even allow the payment of an advance.[91] Access to the preliminary opinion of the court-appointed expert facilitates the victim by giving him/her the choice to push for a settlement, to go to trial or to drop the case.

Germany

Similar to France, the German *Reichszivilprozeßordnung* of 1877 allowed court-appointed expert witnesses (albeit preferring those mutually appointed by the parties)[92] and established the principle of free assessment of the evidence by the judge.[93] The current rules on court-appointed expert witnesses can be found at §§ 402 of the German Code of Civil Procedure, which entered into force in 1900.[94]

Pre-trial orders have been allowed to secure evidence if there is reason to fear that it would be lost or its use made difficult, but their broader use has been questioned.[95]

---

83 C pr civ (1806), arts 302ff.
84 *Loi n° 258 du 15 juillet 1944 sur les rapports d'experts.*
85 *Décret n° 73–1122 du 17 décembre 1973 instituant une quatrième série de dispositions destinées à s'intégrer dans le nouveau code de procédure civile.*
86 C pr civ (1975), arts 232ff.
87 C pr civ (1975), art 246: 'Le juge n'est pas lié par les constatations ou les conclusions du technicien'.
88 Michèle Harichaux, 'L'obligation du médecin de respecter les données de la science (A propos du cinquantenaire de l'arrêt Mercier: bilan d'une jurisprudence)' (1987) JCP G I 3306.
89 Michel Redon, 'Mesures d'instruction confiées à un technicien (Pr. civ.)', *Répertoire de procédure civile Dalloz* (Mise à jour de novembre 2022) para 634 <www-dalloz-fr> accessed 28 July 2023.
90 C pr civ (1975), arts 484–98.
91 C pr civ (1975), art 809 al 2, and nowadays art 835.
92 §§ 376–377 RZPO; McGrath (n 46) 45.
93 § 259 RZPO; McGrath (n 46) 44.
94 *Neubekanntmachung der Civilprozeßordnung vom 30. Januar 1877, RGBl S 83, in der vom 1. Januar 1900 an geltenden Fassung Änderungen (RGBl I S 410).*
95 Martin Rehborn, 'Selbständiges Beweisverfahren im Arzthaftungsrecht?' (1998) (1) MDR 16.

Italy

The Italian Code of Civil Procedure of 1940 allowed the court to appoint an expert to assist the judge whenever necessary,[96] and in that case the parties could appoint their own experts as well.[97] Here, too, the court has discretion over the weight of evidence.[98]

Although the code did not originally envisage pre-trial orders for persons, two decisions of the *Corte costituzionale* (the Italian constitutional court) allowed them.[99] Since 2006, statute law provides that issues of causation and harm regarding the persons can be explored vis-à-vis pre-trial orders,[100] resulting in the broadening of their scope and purpose to include facilitating pre-trial conciliation of the parties.[101]

The Interplay Between Criminal Law and Civil Liability

Another special feature of Continental Law is the interplay between criminal law and civil liability.

Here we will consider only certain offences that doctors can commit against their patients. All the Civil Law systems under consideration require informed consent for medical interference with one's body and freedom, which would be otherwise unlawful. However, leaving aside intentional harm cases, the presence of duly informed consent does not exclude the existence of a criminal offense in the event the treating practitioner, intending to heal the patient, negligently causes death or bodily injury. In these cases, criminal investigations and prosecution are commenced *ex officio*, except for minor injuries (which are investigated and prosecuted only if the patient presses charges against the doctor).

Generally, the victim can be a party in the criminal trial (with the possibility to seek compensation from the defendant) or commence parallel civil proceedings for damages on the same merits.

However, as will be discussed later, the solutions vary considerably from country to country.

France

The old French Criminal Code of 1810 was in force until 1994; its articles 319 and 320 punished *homicide par imprudence* (negligent manslaughter)

---

96 Art 61 c p c.

97 Arts 87, 194 and 201 c p c.

98 Art 116 c p c.

99 Corte cost 22 ottobre 1990 n 471; Corte cost 19 luglio 1996 n 257.

100 Art 2, co 3, lett e-bis, n 5, *decreto legge 14 marzo 2005 n 35 conv con modif in legge 14 maggio 2005 n 80*, which modified art 696 c p c.

101 Art 696-bis c p c.

and *blessures par imprudence* (negligent bodily injuries), respectively, even absent gross negligence.[102] The standard of care was deemed the same under both criminal and private law.[103] The new Criminal Code scarcely modified these crimes, which were punishable under the new articles 221–6 and 222–19.[104]

From a procedural perspective,[105] in addition to the public prosecutor and the defendant, anyone who had suffered harm caused by a crime could be a

---

102 C pén (*ancien*), art 319: 'Quiconque, par maladresse, imprudence, inattention, négligence ou inobservation des règlements, aura commis involontairement un homicide, ou en aura involontairement été la cause, sera puni d'un emprisonnement de trois mois à deux ans, et d'une amende'.

C pén (*ancien*), art 320: 'S'il n'est résulté du défaut d'adresse ou de précaution que des blessures ou coups, l'emprisonnement sera de six jours à deux mois, et l'amende (. . .)', but during the XX century has been repeatedly modified, and this was the result: 'S'il est résulté du défaut d'adresse ou de précaution des blessures, coups ou maladies entraînant une incapacité totale de travail personnel pendant plus de trois mois, le coupable sera puni d'un emprisonnement de quinze jours à un an et d'une amende (. . .) ou de l'une de ces deux peines seulement'.

When the inability to work lasted less than three months, there was the minor offence of C pén (*ancien*), art R 40–4°: 'Seront punis d'un emprisonnement de dix jours à un mois et d'une amende (. . .) ou de l'une de ces deux peines seulement: (. . .) 4. Ceux qui, par maladresse, imprudence, inattention, négligence ou inobservation des règlements, auront involontairement été la cause de blessures, coups ou maladies, n'entraînant pas une incapacité totale de travail personnel supérieure à trois mois'.

103 Penneau (n 37) 163–66.

104 C pén, art 221–6 (*version du 1 mars 1994*): 'Le fait de causer, par maladresse, imprudence, inattention, négligence ou manquement à une obligation de sécurité ou de prudence imposée par la loi ou les règlements, la mort d'autrui constitue un homicide involontaire puni de trois ans d'emprisonnement et de 300 000 F d'amende.

En cas de manquement délibéré à une obligation de sécurité ou de prudence imposée par la loi ou les règlements, les peines encourues sont portées à cinq ans d'emprisonnement et à 500 000 F d'amende'.

C pén, art 222–19 (*version du 1 mars 1994*): 'Le fait de causer à autrui, par maladresse, imprudence, inattention, négligence ou manquement à une obligation de sécurité ou de prudence imposée par la loi ou les règlements, une incapacité totale de travail pendant plus de trois mois est puni de deux ans d'emprisonnement et de 200 000 F d'amende.

En cas de manquement délibéré à une obligation de sécurité ou de prudence imposée par la loi ou les règlements, les peines encourues sont portées à trois ans d'emprisonnement et à 300 000 F d'amende'.

See also C pén, art 222–20 (*version du 1 mars 1994*): 'Le fait de causer à autrui, par un manquement délibéré à une obligation de sécurité ou de prudence imposée par la loi ou les règlements, une incapacité totale de travail d'une durée inférieure ou égale à trois mois, est puni d'un an d'emprisonnement et de 100 000 F d'amende'.

And the minor offence of C pén, art 625–2 (*version du 1 mars 1994*): 'Hors le cas prévu par l'article 222–20, le fait de causer à autrui, par maladresse, imprudence, inattention, négligence ou manquement à une obligation de sécurité ou de prudence imposée par la loi ou les règlements, une incapacité totale de travail d'une durée inférieure ou égale à trois mois est puni de l'amende prévue pour les contraventions de la 5e classe'.

105 Mélinée Kazarian, Danielle Griffiths and Margaret Brazier, 'Criminal Responsibility for Medical Malpractice in France' (2011) 27(4) PN 188, 195.

party in the criminal trial and request damages.[106] Since 1977, subject to some conditions, the state would indemnify the victim who did not receive effective and sufficient compensation from the liable party.[107]

The patient could of course bring a separate civil action instead. However, if a subsequent criminal trial started on the same merits, the civil trial had to be stayed until a final criminal decision[108] resulting in *res judicata* was reached, which applied – at least theoretically – also to private law liability issues.[109]

It must further be observed that the victims were allowed to participate also in those criminal trials in which the courts lacked jurisdiction on damages; that is, most of the cases related to treatments performed in public hospitals.[110] Thus, following a conviction of the employee-clinician, the aggrieved party had to petition an administrative tribunal for damages from the employer-healthcare organisation.[111]

Germany

Things were considerably different in Germany. There, the Criminal Code punished *fahrlässige Tötung* (negligent manslaughter) and *fahrlässige Körperverletzung* (negligent bodily injury) at § 222 and § 229, respectively.[112] However, the right of the victim to claim damages in the criminal trial was introduced only in 1943.[113]

Additionally, scholars have observed that, in Germany, criminal liability requires *Vorwerfbarkeit* (reproachability or subjective culpability), which is more difficult to ascertain compared to objective negligence or non-performance of an obligation under private law.[114]

---

106 C pr pén, arts 2 and 3.
107 *Loi n° 5 du 3 janvier 1977*, which inserted C pr pén, art 706-3, which was modified through *loi n° 589 du 6 juilleet 1990*.
108 C pr pén, art 4 (*version du 8 avril 1958*).
109 Antonio Gambaro, 'Azione civile e processo penale. Appunti di diritto comparato' (1977) Resp Civ Prev 387, 394–97.
110 Yvonne Lambert-Faivre, 'L'éthique de la responsabilité' (1998) RTDCiv 1.
111 Gabriel Blancher, 'Faut-il dépénaliser la responsabilité médicale?' (2001) 185 Bulletin de l'Académie nationale de médecine 1717, 1720.
112 § 222 StGB: 'Wer durch Fahrlässigkeit den Tod eines Menschen verursacht (. . .)'.
   § 229 StGB: 'Wer durch Fahrlässigkeit die Körperverletzung eines Anderen verursacht (. . .)'. Today, this article refers to 'die Körperverletzung einer anderen Person'. Originally, the *Strafgesetzbuch für das Deutsche Reich vom 15. Mai 1871* (the Criminal Code of the German Empire) punished *fahrlässige Körperverletzung* under § 230 and issued for both §§ 222 and 230 a more severe punishment if the perpetrator was particularly obliged to pay attention by virtue of his office, profession or trade, which was repealed in 1940.
113 The *Dritte Verordnung zur Vereinfachung der Strafrechtspflege vom 29. Mai 1943 (RGBl I S 342)* introduced §§ 403ff StPO.
114 Erwin Deutsch and Andreas Spickhoff, *Medizinrecht* (7th edn, Springer 2014) 453–54.

Moreover, German public prosecutors had more tools to drop personal injury cases compared to their French and Italian colleagues.[115] For instance, discontinuation without prejudice under § 170 Abs 2 StPO applied when there was no public interest to prosecute a *Privatklagedelikt* (private prosecution offence),[116] among which there was also the *fahrlässige Körperverletzung*; in this case, the victim could independently prosecute the defendant in the criminal trial.[117]

Italy

Negligent manslaughter and negligent bodily injury were criminalised also in Italy, as the Italian Criminal Code of 1930 punished *omicidio colposo* and *lesioni colpose* at articles 589 and 590, respectively.[118] Similarly to France, requests for damages in criminal proceedings were allowed,[119] separate civil trials had to be stayed until a final criminal decision was reached,[120] and this, at least theoretically, would amount to *res judicata* also on the issue of the commission of a tort.[121]

In 1988, a new Code of Criminal Procedure was adopted,[122] according to which it is not necessary to stay civil proceedings for damages commenced prior to the issuance of a criminal judgement on the same facts.[123] Here, acquittal does not produce *res judicata* on the issue of civil liability,[124] which can be nevertheless found by the civil court. If the victim failed to file

---

115 On the introduction of the special interest clause in the German Criminal Code, see Joachim Herrmann, 'The Rule of Compulsory Prosecution and the Scope of Prosecutorial Discretion in Germany' (1973) 41 UChLRev 468, 480 fn 63.

116 Ralph Kölbel, 'StPO § 170', Rn. 21–22, in Christoph Knauer, Hans Kudlich and Hartmut Schneider (eds), *Münchener Kommentar zur StPO* (Beck 2016).

117 § 374 Abs 1 n 4 StPO; §§ 376–77 StPO; nn 86–87, 89 RiStBV.

118 Art 589 c p (*in vigore fino al 6 giugno 1966*): '[I.] Chiunque cagiona, per colpa, la morte di un uomo è punito con la reclusione da sei mesi a cinque anni'.

Art 590 c p (*in vigore fino al 6 giugno 1966*): 'Chiunque cagiona ad altri, per colpa, una lesione personale è punito con la reclusione fino a tre mesi o con la multa fino a lire cinquemila.

[II.] Se la lesione è grave, la pena è della reclusione da uno a sei mesi o della multa da lire duemila a diecimila; se è gravissima, della reclusione da tre mesi a due anni o della multa da lire cinquemila a ventimila. (. . .)

[IV.] Nel caso preveduto dalla prima parte di questo articolo, il colpevole è punito a querela della persona offesa'.

With *legge 11 maggio 1966 n 296* the wording of the two articles has been modified: for what it concerns our research, it can be noticed that afterwards art 589 c p punished 'Chiunque cagiona per colpa la morte di una persona', and fines in art. 590 c p were increased.

119 Art 22 c p p (1930).

120 Art 24, co 2 c p p (1930).

121 Art 25 c p p (1930); art 27, co 1 c p p (1930); Gambaro (n 109) ibid.

122 *Decreto del Presidente della Repubblica 22 settembre 1988 n 447.*

123 Art 75, co 3 c p p.

124 Art 652 c p p, as amended by art 9 *legge 27 marzo 2001, n 97.*

a timely separate civil action, or if s/he claimed damages in the criminal proceedings, acquittal may also exclude civil liability.[125] Final convictions create *res judicata* regarding the occurrence of the pleaded facts and whether the defendant committed a criminal offence,[126] so that it is very likely that s/he will be held liable also for damages in a subsequent civil trial.

However, for decades the courts subjected the criminal liability of doctors to the establishment of *colpa grave* (gross negligence) – a condition only abandoned at the end of the XX century.[127]

Some Available Data

After having briefly explored the idea of medical malpractice crises and recalled the French, German and Italian legal frameworks before the reforms, we turn now to a quantitative analysis.

This kind of approach was quite rare among civilians. However, some information is available from various sources, allowing us to construct a mosaic of the insurance and litigation contexts in the aforementioned Civil Law systems.

France

Liability insurance was not mandatory for French hospitals, and self-retention was the option for a very relevant player. Specifically, in 1993 the *Assistance Publique* (ie the public body entrusted with healthcare in the Paris area) budgeted for malpractice damages in the aggregate amount of $2 million for all its 50 hospitals, 12,000 physicians and 840,000 admissions per year.[128]

According to the then Director for Regulation and Administrative Litigation Department of the *Assistance Publique*, damages claims by victims totalled 173 in 1988, 237 in 1993 and 259 in 1994,[129] which is 50% more than in 1988.

Other scholars refer to more detailed data from the *Assistance Publique* regarding the period from 1987 to 1991:[130] new filings were 400 in 1987,

---

125 ibid.

126 Art 651 c p p.

127 Pier Francesco Poli, *La colpa grave* (Giuffrè Francis Lefebvre 2021) 77ff.

128 Isabelle Durand-Zaleski, Jean-François Moreau, Elisabeth Conge and Claudine Blum-Boisgard, 'Medical Malpractice in France: The Effects of a Two-Fold Jurisdiction and the Case of Radiology' (1993) 28 Inves Radiol 459, 460.

129 Alain Levasseur, 'Les transactions: l'exemple de l'Assistance publique-Hôpitaux de Paris' (1997) AJDA 54.

130 Christine Le Clainche and Guy Poquet, *La responsabilité médicale et l'indemnisation du risque thérapeutique: Etat des lieux* (Centre de Recherche pour l'Étude et l'Observation des Conditions de Vie – CRÉDOC 1992) 23–24 <www.credoc.fr/download/pdf/Rapp/R128.pdf> accessed 4 July 2023; Dominique Thouvenin, *La responsabilité médicale: Analyse des données*

of which 242 (60.5%) were mere notifications of potential accidents by the hospitals, and 158 (39.5%) were actual claims from the victims; in 1988, these numbers increased to 262 (60.22%) and 173 (39.77%), respectively; in 1989, they were 261 (57.87%) and 190 (42.13%), respectively; in 1990, 227 (56.75%) and 173 (43.25%), respectively; and in 1991, they were 227 (56.47%) and 175 (43.53%), respectively. So, during the 1980s, the filings (ie both notifications by hospitals and claims from victims) were consistently around 400 annually, but the number of claims increased slightly over time.

From the same dataset one can calculate that between 1987 and 1991 there were an average of 56 settlements reached and 74 new litigated cases per year.[131] The Director also stated that, in 1994, only 40 cases were settled, whereas 150 were brought before administrative tribunals; the year 1995, when 449 claims for damages were made, was deemed special, partially because of a new judgment holding hospitals liable in tainted blood cases.[132] It must further be observed that the number of cases brought before administrative tribunals in 1994 doubled compared to the 1987–91 period.

The participation in mutual insurance companies became very common for other public hospitals during the XX century. For instance, *SHAM – Société Hospitalière d'Assurances Mutuelles* – insured around 40% of the market in 1995.[133]

Liability insurance was not mandatory for doctors, either. Nonetheless, in 1991 at least 60% of French doctors were covered by mutual insurance.[134] That year the President of *Le Sou Médical* and an actuarial of the same company, referring to data from the whole *Groupe des assurances mutuelles médicales* (GAMM), a coinsurance partnership between their carrier and the *Mutuelle d'assurances du corps de santé français* (MACSF), stated that the frequency of claims decreased from approximately 1.4% in 1982 to 1% in 1985 before increasing to around 1.7% in 1987, ending at around 1.6% in 1988 and 1989.[135] According to a 2010 article, the incidence of claims per 100 doctors at '*Sou Médical groupe MACSF*' in 1997 was well above 1.5%, and it went to 2% in 2000.[136] Therefore, the 2000 frequency had increased compared to the 1980s, but not significantly.

statistiques disponibles et des arrêts rendus par la Cour de cassation et le Conseil d'Etat de 1984 à 1992 (Flammarion Médicine-Sciences 1995) 17.

131 Le Clainche and Poquet (n 130) 23; Thouvenin (n 130) 16–17.
132 Levasseur (n 129).
133 Thouvenin (n 130) 15 fn 25.
134 Jacques Pouletty and Philippe Sarica, 'La responsabilité civile professionnelle médicale: une approche statistique' (1991) 6 Risques 43 <www.revue-risques.fr/wp-content/uploads/Risques-006_Web.pdf> accessed 4 July 2023.
135 ibid 45.
136 A Najaf-Zadeha, F Dubosa, M Aurela, C Bons-Letouzeyc, R Amalbertic and A Martinot, 'Incidence des déclarations de plaintes envers les pédiatres' (2010) 17(2) Archives de pédiatrie 183.

Further publications distinguish between the requests for compensation by victims and the mere notifications of possible bodily injuries sent by the insured doctors.

The Secretary General of GAMM and Medical Director of *Le Sou Médical*, in a 1998 article referring to the notifications of possible bodily injuries by the insured doctors, stated that their frequency in 1987 was just 1%, and that it was 1.50% in 1996;[137] similarly, a lawyer from *Le Sou Médical* stated that the frequency of the notifications sent by the insured doctors in 1998 was 1.81%–83% higher than in 1988,[138] when it should have therefore been at around 1%. In 1992, at the request of the *Institut national de la consommation*, ie the public body entrusted with consumer information, a private research centre assessed French medical malpractice by analysing, among other things, data from *Le Soi Médical* and MACSF: according to this study, in 1991, there were 2,676 notifications and 114,500 insured doctors,[139] which yields a 2.33% frequency.

Still, a scholar commenting on early GAMM data noticed there were fewer requests by victims for compensation compared to notices of potential accidents sent by doctors to their insurance companies and pointed out that such discrepancy has several possible explanations, including increased caution of the carriers.[140]

In particular, GAMM stated that the requests from the victims and their families rose by 18% between 1980 and 1989, going from 800 to 950;[141] in 1991, they were 1,300;[142] in 1980, GAMM insured 68,000 doctors[143] and stated that in 1989 they were 65% more,[144] ie 112,200 becoming 114,500 in 1991.[145] This means that the number of requests per 100 insured doctors was 1.18 in 1980, 0.85 in 1989 and 1.13 in 1991. Accordingly, the frequency of requests from the victims actually decreased in the 1980s, and in 1991 was slightly below the 1980 level. We also notice that notifications from doctors were always more frequent than the requests from the victims, being 1.64 per 100 doctors in 1980,[146] around 1 in 1988 and then 2.33 in 1991.

---

137 Christian Sicot, 'Responsabilité médicale: l'expérience du groupe des assurances mutuelles médicales (GAMM)' (1998) 182 Bulletin de l'Académie nationale de médecine 541.

138 Germain Decroix, 'Responsabilité médicale en France: mythes et réalité' (2000) 32 ADSP 48, 49 <www.hcsp.fr/Explore.cgi/Telecharger?NomFichier=ad324853.pdf> accessed 4 July 2023.

139 Le Clainche and Poquet (n 130) 13–14.

140 Thouvenin (n 130) 12–14.

141 Pouletty and Sarica (n 134) 44.

142 Le Clainche and Poquet (n 130) 14.

143 Thouvenin (n 130) 13.

144 Pouletty and Sarica (n 134) 43.

145 Le Clainche and Poquet (n 130) 14.

146 Thouvenin (n 130) 14.

The Secretary General of GAMM stated that the average cost of claims in 1996 was 42% higher than in 1985.[147] Some authors referred to content of certain reports from the *Commission de contrôle des assurances*, a public body with supervising powers in France, according to which the average cost of the settlement of insurance claims in the medical malpractice field increased by 50% in the 1990s.[148] The medical malpractice path seems to be different from that of other liability sectors, provided that overall liability insurance costs, according to French economists, increased from 3.0% to 3.4% of the GDP between 1990 and 1993, and then plateaued at around 3.1% in 1996.[149]

In 1998, GAMM reported that, from all the notifications received of potential accidents, just 25% of its closed files resulted in payment in favour of the patients or their relatives.[150] This seems in line with the previous assertions about the 1977–89 period.[151] In detail, as regards the period between 1977 and 1991, 5,081 files were closed: 2,813 (55%) out-of-court, of which 822 were settled with a payment; 1,561 (31%) were civil trials, out of which only 327 ended with a payment; 707 (14%) referred to criminal trials, but just 99 of them brought both conviction and damages;[152] accordingly, insurance payments derived from an out-of-court settlement 7 out of 10 times;[153] 70.78% of the extra-judicial negotiations, 79.05% of the civil trials and 86% of the criminal proceeding ended without payment, respectively. Also, 50.39% of the criminal complaints were not followed by a prosecution. The 1992 update concerning 5,591 closed files showed very similar data.[154] As of 1998, with regard to 9,817 closed files, some of these figures remained almost unchanged: 76.1% of the files was closed without payment, 16% with a payment after a settlement (16.44% as of 1992 and 16.81% as of 1991), 6.2% with a payment after a civil trial (6.46% as of 1992 and 6.43% as of 1991), 1.7% with a criminal conviction (1.98% as of 1992, whereas the 1.95% recorded in 1991 regarded criminal convictions and damages awards).[155]

In the early 1990s, statistics on medical malpractice coming from the judiciary were limited to civil cases,[156] regarding thus only the liability of private hospitals, of their employees and of independent practitioners, while there

---

147 Sicot (n 137) 542.
148 Laurence Helmlinger and Dominique Martin, 'La judiciarisation de la médecine, mythe et réalité' (2004) 5 Les Tribunes de la santé 39, 45.
149 Michel Didier and Peter Taubert, 'Conjoncture de l'assurance et cycle économique' (1998) 33 Risques 33, 36 <www.revue-risques.fr/wp-content/uploads/2019/04/Risques-033_Web.pdf> accessed 5 July 2023.
150 Sicot (n 137) 542.
151 Pouletty and Sarica (n 134) 44.
152 Le Clainche and Poquet (n 130) 18.
153 ibid 19.
154 Thouvenin (n 130) 15.
155 Decroix (n 138) 50.
156 Thouvenin (n 130) VII, 7, 17–18, 24.

was no specific information on their criminal liability; as regards public hospitals, the data concerned only the decisions of final instance.

According to one author, from 1982 to 1987, there were consistently around 300 new civil cases per year concerning the liability of healthcare professionals,[157] increasing to around 550 per year in 1988, when the official classification system underwent some modifications.[158] From 1988 onwards, the applications on the merits were an average of 721 per year at the courts of first instance.[159] The author also informs that in 1992 the average duration of medical malpractice trials was 15.7 months at the *tribunaux de grande instance* (courts for claims of higher value) and 6.8 months at the *tribunaux d'instance* (courts for small value claims), being the average of all civil trials 9.6 and 4.7 months in the respective courts, while the average duration of an appeal was 18.2 months, whereas for the generality of civil controversies was 13.5 months.[160] As regards the outcome, this study refers that in 1992 around 54% of the claims in those courts succeeded at trial, fully or at least in part, and around 20% of them were dismissed.[161]

In 2004, other scholars analysed the same kind of information[162] and found that, from 1990 to 2002, the number of civil trials and interim procedures before the *tribunaux de grande instance* increased fivefold, having been 805 in 1990, 1,112 in 1992, 1,806 in 1994, 2,389 in 1996, 3,221 in 1998, 3,598 in 2000 and 3,906 in 2002.

Meanwhile, the French Ministry of Justice published data on medical malpractice from administrative tribunals of first instance (which, as stated earlier, had jurisdiction on liability cases concerning public hospitals). Specifically, 2,492 suits were filed in 1999, 2,639 in 2000, 2,854 in 2001, 2,955 in 2002, 2,960 in 2003 and 2,707 in 2004.[163] The authors also observed that medical activities increased by 20% between 1990 and 2001.[164]

It has been suggested that the extent of medical malpractice litigation was overestimated by the general public,[165] also taking into consideration the number of medical treatments performed each year in France.[166] However, data from first instance courts clearly indicates an increase in cases, which is considerably more than proportional to the increase in medical treatments.

---

157 ibid 19.
158 ibid 18–19, 20 fn 29.
159 ibid 20.
160 ibid 23–24.
161 ibid 22.
162 Helmlinger and Martin (n 148) 43–44.
163 ibid 44.
164 ibid.
165 Pierre Sargos, 'Réflexions sur les accidents médicaux et la doctrine jurisprudentielle de la Cour de cassation en matière de responsabilité médicale' (1996) D 365, para 8.
166 Helmlinger and Martin (n 148) 44.

Hospital records have also been reviewed in France. According to one study, between August 1978 and August 1979, 12.6% of the admissions to intensive care at the hospital of Crétail were due to iatrogenic disorders, of which 46% were deemed potentially avoidable.[167] Subsequent research conducted in 1994 at the intensive care unit of the hospital of Compiègne found that these rates were 10.9% and 51%, respectively.[168] The same year, anaesthesiologists from Nancy found a 7.37% rate of adverse events,[169] but they did not specify whether these events were preventable.

A prospective cohort study based on total admissions (n=444) to an internal medicine unit over a four-month period found 156 adverse drug reactions in 116 patients (26.1% of total admissions), 80% of which were preventable.[170]

A retrospective study on 870 notifications by insured anaesthesiologists and related claims, both of which were filed between 1986 and 2011 in metropolitan France, found that a probable or certain medical error occurred in 27.5% of cases.[171]

The defensive medicine phenomenon in France seems unexplored prior to the 2002 reforms. A few years later, French sociologists pointed out that the subjective perceived risk of litigation, which is at the core of most studies on defensive medicine, may be unrelated to the actual extent of litigation.[172]

Germany

In 2001, the *Robert Koch Institut* (ie the German government's central scientific institution on biomedicine) estimated 40,000 suspected medical malpractice cases occurred in Germany annually, of which approximately

---

167 Patrick Trunet, Jean-Roger Le Gall and François Lhoste, 'The Role of Iatrogenic Disease in Admissions to Intensive Care' (1980) 244 JAMA 2617, 2618.

168 Bruno Darchy, Eric Le Mière, Bélinda Figueredo, Eric Bavoux and Yves Domart, 'Iatrogenic Diseases as a Reason for Admission to the Intensive Care Unit: Incidence, Causes, and Consequences' (1999) 159 Arch Intern Med 71, 72.

169 B Gravot, JC Pottie, MC Laxenaire, L Feldman, JM Virion and B Legras, 'Evénements indésirables liés à l'anesthésie. Etude prospective d'un an d'activité' (1995) 14 Ann Fr Anesth Réanim R217.

170 R Lagnaoui, N Moore, J Fach, M Longy-Boursier and B Bégaud, 'Adverse Drug Reactions in a Department of Systemic Diseases-Oriented Internal Medicine: Prevalence, Incidence, Direct Costs and Avoidability' (2000) 56 Eur J Clin Pharmacol 181.

171 Mathieu Boutonnet, Pierre Trouiller, Eric Lopard, René Amalberti, Thierry Houselstein, Pierre Pasquier, Yves Auroy and Guillaume De Saint-Maurice, 'Insurance Statements from French Anaesthesiologists and Intensivists: A Database Analysis' (2016) 35 Anaesth Crit Care Pain Med 313, 316.

172 Janine Barbot and Emmanuelle Fillion, 'La «médecine défensive»: critique d'un concept à succès' (2006) 24(2) Sciences sociales et santé 5, 10–11.

12,000 (30%) were confirmed.[173] The following paragraphs will analyse the sources referenced in connection with this conclusion, along with further information.

It must first be recalled that codes of professional conduct adopted in certain *Länder* require German physicians to carry liability insurance.[174]

According to the *Robert Koch Institut*, in 1999, *DBV-Winterthur* (a carrier with 108,000 insured doctors) registered 4,500 claims, approximately 30% of which involved conciliation proceedings, while 10% went to trial; of the cases that went to trial, 4% resulted in a judgment confirming the commission of a treatment error.[175] On average, the DBV-Winterthur is said to have paid 50,000 DM per claim.[176]

The head of medical malpractice at *DBV-Winterthur* reported that in 2001 the number of insured doctors increased to 110,000, with medical malpractice claims (totalling 4,573) accounting for a 6.1% increase compared to the previous year,[177] when they must have thus been around 4,310. The frequency of claims showed a decreasing trend from 1999 to 2002.[178]

Over 93% of claims with alleged personal injury were settled out-of-court; of those brought before a court (7%), 8% were lost (0.56% of all personal injury cases), 34% were settled (2.38%) and 58% won by the company (4.06%); in about one third of all closed claims, expert and conciliation bodies were involved, ending with a payment in 41% of times.[179]

In 2005, *DBV-Winterthur* insured 122,000 physicians and received 4,583 new claims,[180] meaning that claim frequency was lower in 2005 than in 2001. *DBV-Winterthur* was acquired by AXA in 2006, and the following year the portfolios of these two companies were combined with that of the AXA branch, *Deutsche Ärzteversicherung*.[181] Two years later, this company experienced more than a doubling of the loss in the medical malpractice liability class: in 2007, the company recorded € 72.3 million in revenues for premiums, but there was a loss of € 33.8 million; in 2009, these numbers were € 77.8 million and € 77.6 million, respectively, with claims expenses totalling

173 Martin L Hansis and Dieter Hart, 'Medizinische Behandlungsfehler in Deutschland' (4 January 2001) Gesundheitsberichterstattung des Bundes 6–7 <https://edoc.rki.de/bitstream/handle/176 904/3154/24d1rmXbF2ZqM_68.pdf?sequence=1&isAllowed=y> accessed 20 July 2023.

174 Petry (n 47) 241–42.

175 Hansis and Hart (n 173) 6.

176 ibid 7.

177 Patrick Weidinger, 'Aus der Praxis eines Heilwesenversicherers: Aktuelle Entwicklungen in der Arzt- und Krankenhaushaftpflicht' (2004) 22 MedR 289.

178 ibid 290.

179 ibid.

180 Patrick Weidinger, 'Aus der Praxis der Haftpflichtversicherung für Ärzte und Krankenhäuser – Statistik, neue Risiken und Qualitätsmanagement' (2006) 24 MedR 571, 572.

181 Jens Flintrop and Heike Korzilius, 'Arzthaftpflicht: Der Schutz wird teurer' (2010) 107 Dtsch Ärztebl A-692.

€ 155.48 million (ie roughly double the revenue).[182] The chairman of the supervisory board of *Deutsche Ärzteversicherung* admitted that this was not due to an increase in claims' frequency, but rather to the rising costs of the major claims, particularly concentrated in obstetrics.[183] In 2010, *Deutsche Ärzteversicherung* cancelled 65,000 policies and requested higher premiums;[184] for independent gynaecologists performing obstetrical activities, increased premiums exceeded € 40,000.[185]

As German law did not require hospitals to carry medical malpractice insurance, some public healthcare organisations established self-retention systems,[186] while other bought policies.

According to a member of its executive board and head of its claims division, in 1982, *Ecclesia Versicherungsdienst GmbH* (the main insurance broker for hospitals in Germany) received only 538 malpractice claims, while this number increased to 9,748 in 2008;[187] the general frequency of claims cannot be calculated as no information was provided on the number of insured facilities or on its variation during that period.

In a chapter from a book published in 2009, the said member of the executive board stated that *Ecclesia* managed around 900 general liability policies insuring German hospitals.[188] This author also reported that the company performed a long-term study on around 140 acute care facilities, whose policies had been continuously managed by *Ecclesia* since at least 1987: for this sample, reported claims in 1987 totalled 235, and this number increased over the following few years before finally stabilizing at approximately 1,600 per year; the genuine claims have remained constant at about one third of the total,[189] but again no exact figures and timing are given. According to this author, the problem was that a decreasing number of major claims (less than 1% of total registered claims) accounted for around two thirds of the total expenditures, and the situation only worsened between 1987 and 1992 as expenditures increased.[190] It was further stated that courts gradually began issuing greater awards for pain and suffering, life expectancy of the victims

182 Gernot Schlösser, 'Die Arzthaftpflichtversicherung – Daten, Fakten, Zahlen' (2011) 29 MedR 227.
183 ibid.
184 Flintrop and Korzilius (n 181).
185 Schlösser (n 182).
186 Karl Otto Bergmann and Carolin Wever, *Die Arzthaftung: Ein Leitfaden für Ärzte und Juristen* (4th edn, Springer 2014) 227–28.
187 FM Petry, 'Haftpflichtschäden in chirurgischen Abteilungen deutscher Krankenhäuser: Zahlen, Ursachen und Konsequenzen' (2010) 43 Gynäkologe 257.
188 Michael Petry, 'Entwicklung der Schadenaufwendungen im Heilwesenrisiko', in Ilse Dautert and Alexandra Jorzig (eds), *Arzthaftung – Mängel im Schadensausgleich?* (Springer 2009) 93.
189 ibid 95.
190 ibid 95–96.

became longer, and the care for them (especially at home care) became more expensive.[191]

As regards premiums, in 1987, the average premium was € 111 per hospital bed. In years following, this number experienced an upward trend, rising to € 359 until 1995, to € 521 in 2006 and so on.[192]

At least four carriers left the market in 2012,[193] followed by another three companies as of 2015. Thus, hospitals were burdened with an additional premium of about € 230 million overall in the years from 2012 to 2015, while just five insurers remained available for underwriting.[194]

The findings and the arguments made by doctors' and hospitals' insurers resemble and refer to those of the *Gesamtverband der Deutschen Versicherungswirtschaft* (GDV) (the German insurance association), which in 2009 sponsored a research project on the development of serious personal injury in the field of healthcare: 93 major claims recorded from 1995 to 1998 and from 2000 to 2003 by 10 companies covering 80% of the market were analysed, the results of which were summarised in an article. This publication reports that the GDV measured the evolution of the cost of these claims, highlighting that losses increased massively (ie by more than 32%) from the first to the second observation period, going from € 1.3 million to more than € 1.8 million, or almost 6% per year in only five years – more than three times the increase rate in the consumer price index. This was deemed to be attributable to several factors, including growing costs of healthcare services and increased life expectancy of victims. The study further noted that the costs of claims had been underestimated when reserving and suggested that in some cases considerable additional reserving would have been required, which made it extremely difficult to calculate premiums appropriately.[195] Looking to a wider class of 140,000 bodily injury claims of all sizes in the medical sector, the study found that the majority of claims were closed after five settlement years, stating that before 1998 there were still settlement gains while afterwards there were significant settlement losses on average.[196]

One special feature of the German system is the early presence of alternative dispute resolution systems for medical malpractice cases. In April 1975, the *Landesaerztekammer* (the college of physicians) of Bayern and an association of insurers launched the first *Schlichtungsstelle* (conciliation commission). By the end of the same year, the first *Gutachterkommission* (expert

191 ibid 98–101.
192 ibid 97.
193 ibid.
194 FM Petry, 'Versicherbarkeit von Krankenhäusern – ein Problemfeld zunehmender Brisanz' (2015) 48 Gynäkologe 621.
195 Nils Hellberg and Marco Lonsing, 'Dramatische Teuerung von Personenschäden im Heilwesen' (2010) VW 421.
196 ibid.

commission) became operational at the *Aerztekammer Nordrhein*.[197] On a voluntary basis, these bodies offer an evaluation of the case and/or a non-binding decision in medical malpractice disputes.

Since 1979, statistical reports on their activities have been released,[198] and some are referred to by books, law journal articles and official publications. Regarding West Germany, between 1988 and 1991, the commissions received an average of 8.6 applications per 100,000 inhabitants and 27 applications per 1,000 doctors per year.[199] There were 2,258 applications submitted in 1981;[200] 2,853 in 1983;[201] 3,961 in 1985;[202] 4,678 in 1987; 4,904 in 1988;[203] 5,155 in 1990;[204] and 5,619 in 1991.[205] In 1992, the first data from the reunified Germany was released, revealing applications totalled 6,349.[206] Over the years, applications increased, with 7,934 in 1994,[207] 8,189 in 1995,[208] 8,884 in 1997, 11,053 in 2003[209] and finally 11,144 in 2004.[210]

There were 1,283 decisions on the merits in 1981, in which negligence and causation were found 341 times[211] (ie 26.58%). In 1990, there were 3,265 decisions on the merits, of which 779 (ie 23.86%) affirmed negligence and causation.[212]

---

197 Patrick Weidinger, 'Gutachterkommissionen und Schlichtungsstellen aus Sicht eines Arzthaftpflichtversicherers' (2003) VW 674.

198 Bundesärztekammer, *Statistische Erhebung der Gutachterkommissionen und Schlichtungsstellen: Statistikjahr 2006* 1 <www.aerztekammern-schlichten.de/fileadmin/user_upload/_old-files/downloads/Gutachterkommission_Statistik_2006.pdf> accessed 21 July 2023.

199 Hans Georg Krumpaszky, Rolf Sethe and Hans-Konrad Selbmann, 'Die Häufigkeit von Behandlungsfehlervorwürfen in der Medizin' (1997) 48 VersR 420, 422.

200 Bundesministerium für Gesundheit und Soziale Sicherung, *Unterrichtung durch die Bundesregierung. Gutachten 2003 des Sachverständigenrates für die Konzertierte Aktion im Gesundheitswesen: Finanzierung, Nutzerorientierung und Qualität* (2003) 165 <https://dserver.bundestag.de/btd/15/005/1500530.pdf> accessed 24 July 2023.

201 Krumpaszky, Sethe and Selbmann (n 199) 423.

202 Bundesministerium für Gesundheit und Soziale Sicherung (n 200).

203 Krumpaszky, Sethe and Selbmann (n 199) 423.

204 Bundesärztekammer und kassenärztliche Bundesvereinigung, *Qualitätssicherung und kontinuierliche Qualitätsverbesserung: Grundlagen einer bedarfsgerechten Gesundheitsversorgung. Gemeinsame Bestandsaufnahme der Bundesärztekammer und der Kassenärztlichen Bundesvereinigung über die Aktivitäten der Spitzenorganisationen der ärztlichen Selbstverwaltung auf dem Gebiet der Qualitätssicherung in der Medizin 1955 bis 1995* (1996) 18 <www.aezq.de/mdb/edocs/pdf/stellungnahmen/sn-qualitaetssicherung-1996.pdf> accessed 24 July 2023.

205 Krumpaszky, Sethe and Selbmann (n 199) 423.

206 Bundesärztekammer und kassenärztliche Bundesvereinigung (n 204).

207 ibid.

208 Bundesministerium für Gesundheit und Soziale Sicherung (n 200).

209 Manfred Eissler, 'Die Ergebnisse der Gutachterkommissionen und Schlichtungsstellen in Deutschland – Ein bundesweiter Vergleich' (2005) 23 MedR 280.

210 Christina Meurer, *Außergerichtliche Streitbeilegung in Arzthaftungssache* (Springer 2008) 52.

211 ibid.

212 ibid.

Cases that were accepted for a decision on the merits were 3,723 in 1992 and 4,721 in 1994; of these 31.2% and 32.7%, respectively, revealed negligence.[213] No information on causation appears available for these years.

According to one author, the number of issued opinions was 3,636 in 1991, 4,721 in 1994, 5,154 in 1995 and 5,939 in 1996. Furthermore, although negligence was established in around 31% of these cases,[214] nothing is said (again) about causation. However, the information in this article seems partially inconsistent with that reported in a book stating, instead, that in 1995, 7,804 applications were closed, of which 4,454 with an opinion on the merits, finding both negligence and causation in 1,374 (30.85%) cases.[215]

The authors of the *Robert Koch Institut*'s estimation reported that, in 1999, the *Gutachterkommissionen* and the *Schlichtungsstellen* received around 9,800 applications and 6,300 procedures were concluded with an expert opinion; of these, negligence (with or without a subsequent injury) was established about 30% of the time; compared to 1997 numbers, applications in 1999 had increased 10.3%, and decisions rendered by 3.5%.[216]

However, another article stated that overall applications in 1999 totalled 9,545, and that the number of cases accepted for processing had increased from 6,086 in 1997 to 7,686 in 2003, while the negligence ratio decreased slightly during the period, dropping from 0.34 to 0.33.[217] Again, no information on causation is available.

Considering both the data reported in the article and that reported in the aforementioned book,[218] it appears the number of cases accepted for processing matches the number of decisions issued on the merits. According to the same book, these were 6,372 in 2000, 6,901 in 2001, 7,449 in 2002, 7,686 in 2003 and 7,744 in 2004, out of which both negligence and causation have been ascertained in 1,702 (26.71%), 1,686 (24.43%), 1,787 (23.99%), 1,809 (23.54%) and 1,739 (22.46%) cases respectively.[219] For most of these years, some data is available on cases where informed consent is absent, but no information on causation is given.[220]

More detailed and homogeneous annual reports have been made available online from 2006 onwards.[221] An analysis of these records reveals that

---

213 Bundesärztekammer und kassenärztliche Bundesvereinigung (n 204) ibid.
214 Gerhard Neumann, 'Gutachterkommissionen und Schlichtungsstellen: Eine Evaluation der Ergebnisse' (1998) MedR 309, reporting that those of 1996 (n=5939) were 2,303 more than those of 1991.
215 Meurer (n 210).
216 Hansis and Hart (n 173) 5.
217 Eissler (n 209).
218 Meurer (n 210).
219 ibid.
220 ibid.
221 By the Bundesärztekammer, <www.aerztekammern-schlichten.de/statistik> accessed 21 July 2023.

the number of submitted applications was higher in 2004 than in 2005. Afterwards, between 2005 and 2012, the number of the submitted applications increased by 16.70%; first, there was a slight decrease from 10,482 in 2005 to 10,280 in 2006, then a consistent increase to 12,232 in 2012. Decisions on the merits, however, decreased from 7,768 in 2005 to 7,201 in 2006, ending at 7,578 in 2012, with an average of 7,370 per year. There has also been a 12.24% increase in the yearly number of cases in which negligence or lack of informed consent, along with causation, have been found, increasing from 1,683 in 2006 to 1,889 in 2012, no data being available for 2005. These numbers confirm liability has thus always been established in around 16.5% of all decisions issued, and around 24.3% of those issued on the merits. Without considering causation, the commissions found negligence or lack of informed consent in around 29.78% of the opinions on the merits, but for 2005 and 2007 the data from the annual reports is insufficient to calculate this percentage.

The authors of the *Robert Koch Institut*'s estimation correctly observed that, following the opinion by a *Gutachterkommission*, a *Schlichtungstelle* or other public bodies (discussed later), the same case could also go to court.[222] As regards the interplay between the commissions, the insurance carriers and the courts, a dataset of an insurance company showed that as of 1985 about one third of claims had been handled by an expert commission or conciliation board before ultimately settling.[223] And as we already saw, there were similar findings also at the beginning of the XXI century.[224]

According to a 1990 study on the activities of the Nordrhein commission, almost 86% of the cases resulted in an out-of-court settlement.[225] A subsequent survey of liability insurers regarding the opinions of the same commission in 1995 revealed that after 214 findings of malpractice, a lawsuit was filed in 41 cases (19.16%), while out of 483 opinions excluding malpractice there were just 40 (8.28%) lawsuits filed,[226] meaning that of 773 cases examined by the commission, just 10.5% (n=81) went to court, which rejected the opinions of the commission only in five occasions.[227]

A 1998 survey administered to liability insurers regarding the opinions issued in 1992 by the *Norddeutsche Schlichtungsstelle* in Hannover indicated that just 8.6% of the opinions were followed by court proceedings, being confirmed 90% of times.[228]

---

222 Hansis and Hart (n 173) 6.
223 Krumpaszky, Sethe and Selbmann (n 199) 426.
224 Weidinger (n 177) 290.
225 Herbert Weltrich, Lutwin Beck and Ulrich Smentkowski, 'Erfolgreiche Streitschlichtung. Neue Evaluation der Gutachterkommission für ärztliche Behandlungsfehler bei der Ärztekammer Nordrhein – Hohe Quote außergerichtlicher Erledigungen' (1998) (5) Rh ÄBl 10.
226 ibid 11–12.
227 ibid 12–13.
228 Klaus-Dieter Scheppokat and Johann Neu, 'Der Stellenwert von Schlichtung und Mediation bei Konflikten zwischen Patient und Arzt' (2002) 53 VersR 385.

As stated, further players must be considered.

In 2000, § 66 SGB V entered into force, suggesting *Krankenkassen* (health insurance funds) supported insured persons in the pursuit of damages claims for harm caused by faulty private treatments. In 2006, the *Allgemeine Ortskrankenkasse* (AOK), an umbrella organisation of funds, covered 35.52% of the German population and 30.50% of that of Schleswig-Holstein, which in turn was 3.41% of the total.[229] AOK stated to have received, from 2000 to 2005, around 1,700 assistance requests from alleged victims residing in that *Land* (ie around 280 per year), of which approximately 20–30% were treated as medical malpractice cases and 70–80% as complications unattributable to fault.[230]

The funds could also request advice on this topic from the *Medizinische Dienst der Krankenversicherung* (MDK), a public body entrusted with socio-medical advisory and assessment services for the *Krankenkassen*:[231] in Niedersachsen, the number of advisory assignments entrusted to MDK increased considerably between 1994 (n=169) and 2007 (n=2,015),[232] and the complaint rate was unchanged at 20% from 2004 onwards, despite increasing numbers of doctors.[233] The authors of the *Robert Koch Institut*'s estimation reported that MDK issued 9,678 expert opinions in suspected medical malpractice cases, confirming negligence in 24% of them.[234] Since 2009, the main contents of MDK opinions have been recorded in a standardised fashion at the federal level, and annual reports based on this information have been released since 2011.[235] In that year, MDK issued 12,686 opinions nationally, confirming negligence in 32.1% of the cases (n=4,068), 75.1% of which also contained evidence of causation,[236] ie 3,055 medical malpractice cases (24% of the total). The following year, opinions reached 12,483, those confirming negligence were 3,392 (31.5%), and those with evidence of both negligence

---

229 Bundesministerium für Gesundheit, *Statistik über Versicherte, gegliedert nach Status, Alter, Wohnort und Kassenart* (2006) <www.bundesgesundheitsministerium.de/fileadmin/ Dateien/3_Downloads/Statistiken/GKV/Mitglieder_Versicherte/KM6_2006.xls> accessed 14 July 2023.

230 Holger Thomsen, 'Behandlungsfehler und Risikomanagement im AOK-Institut Medizinschaden' (2006) 16 Rechtsmedizin 361, 363–64.

231 § 275(3) S 4 SGB V.

232 Rainer Kirchner and Ralf Lemke, 'Behandlungsfehlerbegutachtung beim MDK Niedersachsen' (2008) 102 ZEFQ 555, 556.

233 ibid 557.

234 Hansis and Hart (n 173) 6.

235 <https://md-bund.de/richtlinien-publikationen/behandlungsfehler.html> accessed 20 July 2023.

236 Ingeborg Singer, Max Skorning and Ingo Kowalski (eds), *Behandlungsfehler-Begutachtung der MDK-Gemeinschaft: Jahresstatistik 2011* (MDS – Medizinischer Dienst des Spitzenverbandes Bund der Krankenkassen e.V., MDK Bayern 2013) 7 <https://md-bund.de/fileadmin/dokumente/ Publikationen/GKV/Behandlungsfehler/Bericht_2011_Behandlungsfehler-Begutachtung_ MDK-Gemeinschaft.pdf> accessed 18 July 2023.

and causation were 21.7% of the total,[237] ie around 2,708 medical malpractice cases. This means that, though slightly decreasing or remaining stationary in 2011–12, the number of issued opinions had actually increased by around 29% since 1999.

At the request of the federal Ministry for Health and Social Affairs, medico-legal scholars published a multicentre retrospective study on 101,358 autopsies performed at 17 out of 33 German institutes of forensic medicine from 1990 to 2000.[238] The study revealed there had been a total of 4,450 alleged lethal malpractice cases related to criminal proceedings,[239] showing a clear increase from 300 in 1990 to more than 600 in 2000,[240] and from 2.38% to 6.68% of all yearly performed autopsies.[241] 3,319 cases were finally clarified, of which 189 (5.7%) featured both negligence and causation.[242] The authors caution that after further investigations, examinations and clinical opinions, the actual number of criminal cases deserving prosecution may be even higher, and that, in any case, often the evidence may have been sufficient for the victim to prevail in civil trial.[243]

Bodily injuries not resulting in death are less frequently related to criminal proceedings, and thus they were seldom brought to the attention of the forensic medicine experts.[244] Nonetheless, these experts noticed a slight but constant increase also in these kinds of cases: they found a total of 434 reports from eight institutes,[245] increasing from 30 in 1990 to more than 45 in 1999, with a peak of more than 75 in 1997;[246] 54 (12.54%) revealed both negligence and causation.[247]

---

237 Ingeborg Singer, Martin Grotz, Heike Klotzbach, Ingo Kowalski, Ralf Lemke, Dimitrios Psathakis and Max Skorning, *Behandlungsfehler-Begutachtung der MDK-Gemeinschaft: Jahresstatistik 2012* (MDS – Medizinischer Dienst des Spitzenverbandes Bund der Krankenkassen e.V., MDK Bayern 2013) 6 <https://md-bund.de/fileadmin/dokumente/Publikationen/GKV/Behandlungsfehler/Bericht_BHF-Begutachtung_2012_final.pdf> accessed 18 July 2023.

238 Johanna Preuß, Reinhard Dettmeyer and Burkhard Madea, *Begutachtung behaupteter letaler und nicht letaler Behandlungsfehler im Fach Rechtsmedizin. Bundesweite multizentrische Studie im Auftrag des Bundesministeriums für Gesundheit und Soziales (BMGS)* (2005) <www.bundesgesundheitsministerium.de/fileadmin/Dateien/5_Publikationen/Ministerium/Begutachtung-Behandlungsfehler-Rechtsmedizin.pdf> accessed 14 July 2023; a summary of the results in English can be found in Burkhard Madea and Johanna Preuß, 'Medical Malpractice as Reflected by the Forensic Evaluation of 4450 Autopsies' (2009) 190 Forensic Sci Int 58.

239 Preuß, Dettmeyer and Madea (n 238) 22.

240 ibid 27–32.

241 ibid 25.

242 ibid 57, 136.

243 ibid 136–37, 147–48.

244 ibid 112, 114.

245 ibid 113.

246 ibid 111.

247 ibid 134.

Unfortunately, no information about the totality of the decisions of the courts for these cases was available.[248] However, a year later, a study limited to the assignments of the Institute of Forensic Medicine of the University of Bonn between 1989 and 2003 showed that 87% of 210 preliminary criminal proceedings were either closed with discontinuance under § 170 Abs 2 StPO or an acquittal verdict was reached, and just 7.6% were either completed under § 153a Abs. 1 StPO (ie a waiver of prosecution subject, for example, to the payment of damages to the victim), or resulted in conviction.[249] These outcomes are similar to those of several other studies.[250]

Limited information about civil trials in Germany is available, because official statistics on medical malpractice cases have been collected only since 2004.[251]

According to a study, between 1977 and 1987 the average frequency of civil complaints against hospitals in Bremen was 12.4 per 100,000 treated patients, 5.8 per 1,000 doctors per year, and 46% of the lawsuits ended with either a decision in favour of the claimant or with a settlement. However, looking also to other publications, it has been estimated more generally that patients were successful in about 50% of their lawsuits before civil courts.[252] The Bremen study additionally reported an average lag of 30 months between the occurrence of the harm and the filing of the lawsuit, and that medical malpractice trials lasted about three times longer than all the other civil proceedings (16.4 versus 6 months), while the duration of medical malpractice appeals was double of those on other civil matters (11 versus 5.4 months).[253]

The data collected at the national level between 2004 and 2011 showed an increase in medical malpractice cases decided by the *Landgericht* from 5,265 to 8,861, while at the same time those decided by the *Amtsgericht* decreased: as both are first instance courts but the latter has jurisdiction on claims of a maximum value of € 5,000, a scholar noted that there should have been an increase in the economic value of malpractice claims.[254] Results were similar

---

248 ibid 57, 145.
249 Burkhard Madea, Christoph Vennedey, Reinhard Dettmeyer and Johanna Preuß, 'Ausgang strafrechtlicher Ermittlungsverfahren gegen Ärzte wegen Verdachts eines Behandlungsfehlers' (2006) 131 DMW 2073.
250 Christoph Vennedey, 'Ausgang strafrechtlicher Ermittlungsverfahren gegen Ärzte wegen Verdachts eines Behandlungsfehlers' (PhD thesis, Universität Bonn 2007) 86 <https://bonndoc.ulb.uni-bonn. de/xmlui/bitstream/handle/20.500.11811/2947/1122.pdf?sequence=1> accessed 20 July 2023; Thomas Alexander Peters, *Der strafrechtliche Arzthaftungsprozeß. Eine empirisch-dogmatische Untersuchung in kriminalpolitischer Absicht* (Pro Universitate Verlag 2000); Thomas Alexander Peters, 'Defensivmedizin durch Rechtsunsicherheit im Arztstrafverfahren?' (2003) 21 MedR 219.
251 Statistische Ämter des Bundes und der Länder, *Fachserie. 10, Rechtspflege. Reihe 2, Gerichte und Staatsanwaltschaften. 1, Zivilgerichte* <www.statistischebibliothek.de/mir/receive/DESerie_ mods_00000101> accessed 27 July 2023.
252 Krumpaszky, Sethe and Selbmann (n 199) 424.
253 ibid.
254 Dominique Püster, *Entwicklungen der Arzthaftpflichtversicherung* (Springer 2013) 76.

the following year.[255] It can be further noted that between 2004 and 2012 the average number of medical malpractice cases decided by the German civil courts went from 7,650 to 10,314 per year, which is a 34% increase, with an average of around 9,700 per year.

Some local studies have been performed also after 2004.

In 2009, a total of 130 medical malpractice cases came to an end at the *Landgericht Dortmund*. The patients won in 50 of them (38%) (14 by judgment and 36 by way of settlement) and lost in 80 (62%) (70 by judgment and 10 by withdrawal of claims).[256]

A study on medical malpractice cases at the courts of Kassel and Marburg found that between 2006 and 2010 152 (65.6%) out of 232 ended with a settlement, and only six (2.6%) with a judgment in favour of the claimants.[257]

In 2006, *Aktionsbündnis Patientensicherheit e.V.* (a network for safety joined by different players in healthcare, including professionals' and patients' associations, and working under the auspices of the Federal Ministry of Health) performed a systematic review of 151 studies published between 1995 and 2005 regarding the frequency of adverse events, preventable adverse events, negligent adverse events, errors and near misses, finding just seven of the studies focusing on Germany.[258] The majority of the reported adverse events frequencies ranged between 0.1% and 20%, the frequency of preventable adverse events between 0.1% and 10%, although adverse events' frequency was between 5% and 10% in larger studies.[259] The review concluded that there was no evident difference between the frequency of adverse events and preventable adverse events in Germany and in the international findings.[260]

However, German medico-legal scholars cautioned that data on adverse events should not be read as information on medical malpractice.[261]

There was almost no research on defensive medicine in Germany. A survey administered to residents in neurology showed that students attending German

---

255 Statistisches Bundesamt, *Rechtspflege Zivilgerichte 2012* (2013) 18, 48 <www.statistische bibliothek.de/mir/servlets/MCRFileNodeServlet/DEHeft_derivate_00012135/210021012 7004.pdf> accessed 27 July 2023.

256 Gisela Kothe-Pawel, 'Die Erfolgsaussichten von Klagen in Arzthaftungsprozessen anhand der Ergebnisse vor dem Landgericht Dortmund im Jahr 2009' (2010) 28 MedR 537.

257 Jan-Paul Knaak and Markus Parzeller, 'Court decisions on medical malpractice' (2014) 128 Int J Legal Med 1049, 1051, 1054.

258 Dieter Conen, Ferdinand Gerlach, Daniel Grandt, Dieter Hart, Günther Jonitz, Jörg Lauterberg, Constanze Lessing, Hannelore Loskill, Matthias Rothmund and Matthias Schrappe, *Agenda Patientensicherheit 2006* (Aktionsbündnis Patientensicherheit e.V. 2006) 17 <http://schrappe. com/ms2/index_htm_files/agenda2006.pdf> accessed 27 July 2023.

259 ibid.

260 ibid 18.

261 Burkhard Madea and Elke Doberentz, 'Häufigkeit letaler Behandlungsfehler in deutschen Kliniken' (2015) 25 Rechtsmedizin 179.

medical schools feared litigation less than their American colleagues.[262] Another contribution cleverly highlighted that, unlike independent practitioners, *Vertragsärzte* (physicians whose services are compensated through statutory health insurance funds) were unable to establish their own pricing policy, as their fees depended largely on the provisions of statutes and collective agreements.[263] Therefore, independent practitioners could not offset increased risk of liability or higher premiums with increased individual earnings, and defensive medicine would have thus been an option for them.[264] The article additionally observed more generally that hospital doctors potentially face similar problems.[265] Indeed, this can be said also for many doctors working in the French and Italian healthcare systems.

Italy

In Italy, the *Associazione nazionale fra le imprese assicuratrici* (ANIA) (the national association of insurance companies) is the most referenced source of data on the pre-reform medical malpractice landscape. It collects reports from Italian carriers, but not from foreign companies selling policies in Italy or claims that are managed by hospitals through self-retention systems.

It must also be considered that liability insurance was not mandatory for physicians and hospitals during the XX century, except between 1969 and 1979.[266] Nonetheless, by 1995 half of all doctors and nearly all facilities were insured.[267] Moreover, at the end of the XX century, thanks to collective bargaining, specialists affiliated with the public healthcare system and doctors working as employees of public hospitals received liability insurance as a benefit;[268] in 2005, coverage for the latter class of physicians was

262 Roland Brilla, Stefan Evers, Angela Deutschlander and Katja Elfriede Wartenberg, 'Are Neurology Residents in the United States Being Taught Defensive Medicine?' (2006) 108 Clin Neurol Neurosurg 374.

263 Horst Herzog, 'Zwischen Budget und Haftung – Faktische Rationalisierungsentscheidungen auf dem Rücken der Ärzte' (2007) GesR 8, 9–10.

264 ibid 12.

265 ibid 8.

266 In that period, a formal obligation on hospitals to get insurance for their dependants derived from art 29 *decreto del Presidente della Repubblica 27 marzo 1969 n 130*, which was implicitly abrogated by art 28 *decreto del Presidente della Repubblica 20 dicembre 1979 n 761*, making that cover merely facultative, see Emilia Giusti, 'Assicurazione sanitaria: la legge Balduzzi dopo il d.l. n. 90 del 2014 e alcune riflessioni sul modello autoassicurativo', *Giustiziacivile.com* (5 November 2014) 3–4 <https://giustiziacivile.com/pdfpage/443 > accessed 9 June 2023.

267 Francesco Introna, 'È possibile introdurre l'assicurazione obbligatoria per responsabilità professionale medica?' (1997) Riv It Med Leg 1121, 1126.

268 Art 31 *decreto del Presidente della Repubblica 28 settembre 1990 n 316*; art 24 *Contratto collettivo nazionale di lavoro quadriennio 1998–2001 dell'area della dirigenza sanitaria professionale tecnica ed amministrativa del Servizio Sanitario Nazionale* <www.aranagenzia.it/

extended also to *colpa grave* (gross negligence) at only a slight additional cost for them.[269]

Drawing from a sample of insurance companies, whose revenues from premiums in 2011 accounted for 32% of the entire general third-party liability market, ANIA's report for the years 2012–13 estimated the number of claims filed in Italy for each year between 1994 and 2011: those concerning physicians increased from 3,222 in 1994 to 10,078 in 2000, and those against hospitals from 6,345 to 23,249.[270] These numbers have of course to be matched with those of the insured physicians.

Looking to ANIA's reports, scholars found that between 2000 and 2008, there were around 13–14 claims per 100 physicians, with average paid damages of around 40,000 euros; however, only 20% of claims ended in a lawsuit.[271]

Interestingly, from 2000, car insurance experienced decreased claims frequency while the average cost of claims simultaneously increased.[272]

According to ANIA's 2012–13 estimation, during the first decade of the XXI century, the claims regarding hospitals and those regarding doctors decreased slightly before plateauing at around 30,000 per year.[273] However, analysing the information from AON, Marsh and Willis Italy (the three major international insurance brokers operating in the country from 2004 to 2012), another study estimated an increase in claims over time.[274] The *Istituto per la vigilanza sulle assicurazioni* (IVASS) (the Italian supervisory authority for insurance) also began looking into the medical malpractice liability insurance

contrattazione/aree-dirigenziali/area-iv/contratti/344-ccnl-normativo-1998-2001-economico-1998-1999.html#ART.%2024:%20Coperture%20assicurative> accessed 8 June 2023.

269 Art 21 *Contratto collettivo nazionale di lavoro dell'area della dirigenza dei ruoli sanitario, professionale, tecnico ed amministrativo del servizio sanitario nazionale parte normativa quadriennio 2002/2005 e parte economica biennio 2002–2003* <www.aranagenzia.it/attachments/article/1712/CCNL%203_11_2005_Quad%202002_2005.pdf> accessed 9 June 2023.

270 ANIA, *Italian Insurance 2012–2013* (2013) 126 <www.ania.it/documents/35135/126704/Italian-Insurance-in-2012-2013.pdf/4f2ef508-2dbc-131e-7c40-25cb9e330132?version=1.0&t=1575554686678> accessed 12 June 2023. See also the Italian version of the same document, ANIA, *L'assicurazione italiana 2012–2013* (2013) 222 <https://ania.it/documents/35135/0/Assicurazione-Italiana-2012-2013.pdf/1a921ad3-efd4-6073-50f3-7c05a5770b0b?t=1576519512151> accessed 12 June 2023.

271 Sofia Amaral-Garcia and Veronica Grembi, 'Curb Your Premium: The Impact of Monitoring Malpractice Claims' (2014) 114 Health Policy 139, 140; Sofia Amaral-Garcia and Veronica Grembi, 'Economia della malpractice medica', in Massimo Franzoni (ed), *Le responsabilità nei servizi sanitari* (Zanichelli 2011) 14ff.

272 ANIA, *Italian Insurance 2012–2013* (2013) (n 270) 78.

273 ibid 126.

274 Marco Bonetti, Pasquale Cirillo, Paolo Musile Tanzi and Elisabetta Trinchero, 'An Analysis of the Number of Medical Malpractice Claims and Their Amounts' (2016) 11 PloS One 1, 20 <https://doi.org/10.1371/journal.pone.0153362> accessed 26 May 2023.

market.[275] In 2017, IVASS published for the first time an issue of its statistical bulletin specifically focused on medical malpractice, collecting reports from all carriers authorised to sell general liability insurance in Italy (including those headquartered abroad),[276] also publishing the statistical tables at the basis of the publication.[277] Of the medical malpractice claims received in 2011 (n=28,576), 19,362 concerned hospitals and 9,214 concerned healthcare professionals,[278] which is not far from ANIA's estimation for the same year.[279]

The discrepancy between the ANIA and foreign carriers' estimations on claims trends is likely due to a shift from national to foreign insurance companies, which is confirmed by IVASS.

Indeed, since 1990, medical malpractice insurance was deemed almost unprofitable.[280] The oldest data available from IVASS (regarding 2010, 2011 and 2012) indicates a loss ratio consistently above 100%, ending with 115.7% for 2012; however, when it comes to health professionals, this ratio was between 88% and 100%.[281]

Notably, other liability fields were less problematic for the Italian carriers. According to ANIA, the loss ratio for the overall non-life insurance sector has always been below 80% since 2005, ending at 71.8% for 2012 data.[282] Similarly, car insurance has always been below 90%, being 74.1% for 2012.[283]

The IVASS 2015 general report indicated that from 2010 to 2014, Italian carriers and branches of non-EU carriers operating in Italy scored −72.59% in premiums collected from hospitals, whereas carriers from the European Economic Area operating in Italy scored +3.21%.[284] According to ANIA, in 2016, public hospitals paid 95% of premiums to four companies, three of which were foreign.[285]

275 IVASS, *Report on the Activities Pursued by IVASS in the Year 2014* (2015) 127 ff <www. ivass.it/pubblicazioni-e-statistiche/pubblicazioni/relazione-annuale/2015/RELAZIONE_ IVASS_2014_en.pdf?language_id=3> accessed 29 December 2023.

276 IVASS, 'Healthcare Liability Risks in Italy 2010–2016' (2017) IV(14) Statistical Bullettin 6 < www.ivass.it/pubblicazioni-e-statistiche/statistiche/bollettino-statistico/2017/n14/report_ italian_medmal_2017.pdf?language_id=3> accessed 29 December 2023.

277 IVASS, *Tavole statistiche r.c. sanitaria 2010–2016* (2017) <www.ivass.it/pubblicazioni-e-statistiche/statistiche/bollettino-statistico/2017/n14/RC_SANITARIA.XLSB?force_ download=1> accessed 13 June 2023.

278 ibid tab A.4.

279 ANIA, *Italian Insurance 2012–2013* (n 270) 126, that figured 2,568 more claims against doctors and 265 fewer claims against hospitals.

280 Introna (n 267) 1126.

281 IVASS (n 277) tab A.12.

282 ANIA, *Italian Insurance 2012–2013* (n 270) 69.

283 ibid 73.

284 IVASS (n 275) 129.

285 Sergio Desantis and Gianni Giuli (eds), *ANIA Trends. Focus R.C. sanità* (2017) 2 <www.ania. it/documents/35135/53795/Ania-Trends-Focus-RC-Sanitaria.pdf/6a0f70f9-90cf-2572-aca8-4ceed26f7bab?version=1.0&t=1573729011189> accessed 12 June 2023.

Another shift justifies the apparently decreasing trend of claims in ANIA's estimation: a shift from insurance to risk retention, which regarded hospitals and is confirmed by multiple sources. At the end of the first decade of the XXI century, no specific data on coverage availability seems to have been collected.[286] However, some indirect evidence of the growing difficulty with finding policies for healthcare facilities was already present. Analysing data from the Ministry of Health, the Italian National Institute of Statistics and the Ministry of Justice, researchers found that in 2008 the average premium for most facilities exceeded double that of 2001, whereas legal expenses increased even more.[287] Peaks of the variation of premiums have been registered in 1995, 1999 and 2000, but their reasons remain uncertain.[288] In Emilia-Romagna, between 2000 and 2004 there were 17% fewer claims despite an overall 137% increase in premiums, which soared from € 18.4 million to € 43.7 million.[289] Some years later, also in Toscana, the yearly premiums paid were ca 50 million euros, whereas compensation amounted to just 5–6 million.[290] And by 2014, only the Val d'Aosta Region and the Province of Bolzano had not yet opted for full risk retention systems or policies with considerable self-insured retention clauses.[291]

This shift towards self-retention is also evident from the insurance market perspective: according to the IVASS 2015 general report, from 2010 to 2014 hospitals scored −43.3% in premiums and the Herfindahl-Hirschman supply concentration index went from 2,438 up to 4,452.[292] The 2017 bulletin from the same institution stated that in 2016 public facilities with an insurance policy were half of those in 2010, private hospitals scored −23.8%, while the average premium was 393,813 euros and 22,204 respectively, both values being higher compared with those of 2010 (respectively by 7.5% and 53.7%).[293]

The 10-year limitation period for contractual liability deserves to be compared with the overall average delay between the adverse event and the

286   Amaral-Garcia and Grembi, 'Economia della malpractice medica' (n 271) 35–39.
287   Amaral-Garcia and Grembi, 'Curb Your Premium: The Impact of Monitoring Malpractice Claims' (n 271) 143 and online Appendix, Tables A4-A5.
288   Amaral-Garcia and Grembi, 'Economia della malpractice medica' (n 271) 35–39.
289   Francesco Taroni and Alberto Cicognani, 'L'istituzionalizzazione del governo del rischio nel servizio sanitario nazionale ed il ruolo della medicina legale' (2007) Riv It Med Leg 1329, 1332.
290   Gian-Aristide Norelli, Federica De Luca, Martina Focardi, Raffaella Giardiello and Vilma Pinchi, 'The Claims Management Committees Trial: Experience of an Italian Hospital of the National Health System' (2015) 29 J Forensic Legal Med 6, 7.
291   Gianluca Romagnoli, 'Autoassicurazione della responsabilità medica: compatibilità con i principi di diritto interno ed europeo' (2015) Danno e Resp 329, 330.
292   IVASS (n 275) 129, 131.
293   IVASS (n 276) 10.

following claim, which is just 1.69 years in the international insurance brokers dataset,[294] or 23.42 months according to a study on 2,144 insurance claims over the 2004–10 period regarding 10 public healthcare organisations operating in one undisclosed Italian region (which also confirmed that the number of claims has indeed increased during that period).[295] According to a study on civil suits against Orthopaedics and Traumatologists in Rome, the average lag between the event and the claim was 3.2 years, followed by further 3.8 years of trial.[296] Research on radiologists indicated that by the fifth year following the event, 98% of the claims were filed, but claims for failure to diagnose cancer tended to be filed 3 or more years after the event.[297] Information from Emilia-Romagna on this topic regards the 2008–11 period, when 91% of the claims were filed by the fifth year following the event, with an average time of 656 days.[298] However, the Lombardia dataset, which gets back to a decade earlier, shows an increasing average time, which was 472 days in 1999, and 710 days in 2010.[299]

Although Italian medico-legal scholars were aware of US hospital records studies, it seems that similar research could not be performed in Italy during the 1990s due to the still paper-based nature of the Italian healthcare organisations and other restraints.[300] However, reviewing their individual or small group activities, already in the 1980s, Italian medico-legal experts and coroners experienced an increase in assignments related to medical malpractice investigations and in the number of their witness testimonies in trials concerning healthcare professionals.[301] Most of these reviews found negligence

---

294 Norelli, De Luca, Focardi, Giardiello and Pinchi (n 290) 8.

295 Luigi Buzzacchi, Giuseppe Scellato and Elisa Ughetto, 'Frequency of Medical Malpractice Claims: The Effects of Volumes and Specialties' (2016) 170 Soc Sci Med 152, 156, 158.

296 Umberto Tarantino, Alessio Giai Via, Ernesto Macrì, Alessandro Eramo, Valeria Marino and Luigi Tonino Marsella, 'Professional Liability in Orthopaedics and Traumatology in Italy' (2013) 471 Clin Orthop Relat Res 3349, 3352.

297 Adriano Fileni, Nicola Magnavita, Paoletta Mirk, Ivo Iavicoli, Giulia Magnavita and Antonio Bergamaschi, 'Radiologic Malpractice Litigation Risk in Italy: An Observational Study Over a 14-Year Period' (2010) 194 Am J Roentgenol 1040, 1042.

298 Regione Emilia-Romagna, *Report Sinistri del Servizio sanitario della Regione Emilia-Romagna Quadriennio 2008–2011 e aggiornamenti 2012* (2014) 45 <https://assr.regione.emilia-romagna. it/pubblicazioni/rapporti-documenti/report-sinistri-ssr-2008-2011-2012/@@download/publica tionFile/report-sinistri-2008-2012.pdf> accessed 14 June 2023.

299 Regione Lombardia and Aon S.p.A. Insurance & Reinsurance Brokers, *Mappatura del rischio del Sistema Sanitario Regionale. Risultati diciassettesima edizione 31/12/2020* (2021) <www. regione.lombardia.it/wps/wcm/connect/7bcf1866-49ab-42cf-93de-2f19d67ecf03/XVII+E dizione+Mappatura+regionale.pdf?MOD=AJPERES&CACHEID=ROOTWORKSPACE-7bcf1866-49ab-42cf-93de-2f19d67ecf03-nQ8.yRB> accessed 13 June 2023.

300 Francesco Introna, 'L'epidemiologia del contenzioso per responsabilità medica in Italia ed all'estero' (1996) Riv It Med Leg 71, 120–21, 123ff, 171, 173–78.

301 ibid 99ff.

in between 30% and 40% of the cases.[302] Subsequently, an analysis of the archive of the Institute of Forensic Medicine of the *Università degli Studi di Milano* on total alleged medical malpractice cases subject to judicial autopsy from January 1996 to December 2009 (n=317) revealed a considerable increase of medico-legal activities in 2001; specifically, alleged malpractice cases every 100 autopsies performed went from 1.29 to 2.14 in 2001, increasing consistently in the following years all the way to 3.86 in 2009.[303] A full forensics report was available only in 71 cases, and there was evidence of negligence and causation in only 12% of them.[304]

As regards inpatient care, a retrospective and multicentre study reviewed the clinical records of the admissions in 5 Italian hospitals in 2008, finding incidences of adverse events on admissions, on average, accounted for 5.2.[305] 93.78% of these events had some consequence for patients, whereas the rest had effects that could be resolved during the hospital stay.[306] Considering those adverse events potentially preventable, with preventability deemed to be at least fairly likely, the study concluded that 56.71% of these events were potentially preventable.[307] The authors caution that it would be inappropriate to transpose the results of their research to the professional liability field, since the study was oriented towards the quality and safety of care.[308]

This admonition can be read as an invitation not to deem adverse events as an obvious or even probable source of liability. In sum, after the reading, we should not speculate on the judicial outcomes, but perhaps we can imagine that adverse events might induce injured patients to at least seek compensation out-of-court. If we consider the incidence of adverse events, select those having a negative consequence on patients, and among them the potentially preventable ones, we can expect that 2.76% of the admitted patients might have had some reasons for filing a claim. If this is true, in 2008 there could have been up to 333,979 claims out of the total number of national discharges

302 ibid 100, 108–11; Nunzio Di Nunno, Alessandro Dell'Erba, Luigi Viola, Luigi Vimercati, Stephen Cina and Francesco Vimercati, 'Medical Malpractice: A Study of Case Histories by the Forensic Medicine Section of Bari' (2004) 25 Am J Forensic Med Pathol 141, 142.

303 Michelangelo B Casali, Francesca Mobilia, Sara Del Sordo, Alberto Blandino and Umberto Genovese, 'The Medical Malpractice in Milan-Italy: A Retrospective Survey on 14 Years of Judicial Autopsies' (2014) 242 Forensic Sci Int 38, 39.

304 ibid 41.

305 Riccardo Tartaglia, Sara Albolino, Tommaso Bellandi, Elisa Bianchini, Annibale Biggeri, Giancarlo Fabbro, Luciana Bevilacqua, Alessandro Dell'Erba, Gaetano Privitera and Lorenzo Sommella, 'Eventi avversi e conseguenze prevenibili: studio retrospettivo in cinque grandi ospedali italiani' (2012) 36 Epidemiol Prev 151.

306 ibid 158.

307 ibid 157.

308 ibid 160.

(which was 12,100,698).[309] But according to ANIA's estimations, only 29,597 medical malpractice claims were filed that year, of which 17,746 concerned hospitals and 11,851 healthcare professionals.[310]

A review of the records of a hospital in Veneto showed an increase from around 70 claims opened in 1999 to 130 claims in 2003, then they declined and increased again to around 120 in 2009; 73% started with an extra-judicial request for compensation, whereas 13% with a civil lawsuit and 17% with criminal proceedings;[311] 858 out of 1,004 files contained sufficient data for an assessment by the medico-legal unit of the hospital itself, with liability established in 31% of the cases.[312]

None of the aforementioned retrospective reviews matched their results with the actual outcomes of judicial decisions or with payments made by the insurers.

It is difficult to gather information from the Italian courts about medical malpractice litigation in the XX century, as the digitalisation of Italian court dockets and decisions came later.[313]

Funded by the *Provincia Autonoma di Trento* and with the auspices of the local college of physicians, a research team from the *Univeristà degli Studi di Trento* Law School combed the paper-based archives of the Trento court of appeals and those of the most relevant courts of first instance in its circuit, looking for civil and criminal decisions issued from 1980 to 2002 in medical malpractice cases, and they found around 120 of them, which they deemed a small but significant sample.[314] Specifically, there were no decisions issued in civil cases before 1986, there were 2 in 1987, only 1 in 1988, 2 each year from 1989 to 1993, 6 in 1994, 3 in 1995, 11 in 1996, 7 in 1997, 8 in 1998, 4 in 1999 and 8 in 2000 (ie 60 cases overall),[315] with an average duration of 4

---

309 Ministero della Salute, *Rapporto annuale sull'attività di ricovero ospedaliero. Dati SDO 2008* (2009) 2 <www.salute.gov.it/imgs/C_17_pubblicazioni_1253_allegato.pdf> accessed 16 June 2023.

310 ANIA, *Italian Insurance 2012–2013* (n 270) 126.

311 Anna Aprile, Matteo Bolcato, Lucrezia Denise Fabbri, Silvia Pagan and Daniele Rodriguez, 'Analisi e valutazione medico-legale di 1004 casi di responsabilità professionale in ambito sanitario' (2013) Riv It Med Leg 93, 96.

312 ibid 101–03.

313 Veronica Grembi and Nuno Garoupa, 'Delays in Medical Malpractice Litigation in Civil Law Jurisdictions: Some Evidence from the Italian Court of Cassation' (2013) 8 Health Econ Policy L 423, 424.

314 Umberto Izzo and Giovanni Pascuzzi (eds), *La responsabilità medica nella Provincia Autonoma di Trento: Il fenomeno. I problemi. Le possibili soluzioni* (Giunta della Provincia Autonoma di Trento 2003) 27–28, 31, 217–18, 220 fn 7: starting from those issued from 1 January 1980 on-wards, the research analysed the civil decisions issued until June 2001 and the criminal decisions issued until June 2002; the research did not consider all the *Preture* having offices in the Trento Province, ie courts of first instance with jurisdiction on civil claims up to 50,000,000 £ and on crimes with a maximum sentence of 3 years of imprisonment.

315 ibid 31, 390–91.

years and 10 months at the trial stage and 2 years and 7 months in appeal.[316] Additionally, there were a total of 57 criminal decisions, which appeared a bit earlier but followed a trend similar to the civil decisions, with 1 criminal decision in 1980, 2 in 1981, 2 in 1983, 3 in 1984, 2 in 1985, 2 in 1986, 1 in 1987, 4 in 1991, 2 in 1992, 4 in 1993, 1 in 1994, 2 in 1995, 4 in 1997, 1 in 1998, 7 in 1999, 5 in 2000, 9 in 2001 and 5 in the first half of 2002.[317] Criminal trials lasted on average 3 years and 1 month at trial and 2 years and 1 month in appeal starting from the date of the event (ie the day the crime was committed).[318]

From the qualitative analysis of the cases,[319] it is possible to deduce that the court ruled in favour of the defendants in 20 civil and 27 criminal proceedings; focusing on criminal procedures, there were 4 plea bargains and 14 dropped charges, which may happen for *lesioni colpose* when an out-of-court settlement on damages has been reached.

The same authors have also been granted access to data from the *Azienda provinciale per i Servizi Sanitari*, which was the only public body organising healthcare services in the *Provincia di Trento*.[320] According to these records, files on 398 claims were collected from 1997 to 2001–59 in 1997, 79 in 1998, 84 in 1999, 88 in 2000 and 88 the following year, thus illustrating an increase.[321] Of these claims, 59 claims resulted in civil proceedings and 43 in criminal proceedings;.[322] Additionally, 7 claims were followed by both a civil and a criminal action.[323]

Accessing a specific informatic archive,[324] a joint venture project between the court of Rome, the local college of physicians and the Law School of *Università degli Studi 'Tor Vergata'* analysed all the civil decisions issued in that forum from 2001 to 2007. The results were published in a law journal article, according to which: 1,938 decisions involving 2,223 doctors were issued during that period;[325] defendants prevailed in 32% of the cases; 56% of the claims were fully successful; 12% of them at least partially successful; the judicial opinions agreed with court-appointed

---

316 ibid 394.
317 ibid 31–32, 392–93.
318 ibid 389, 395.
319 ibid 221–318.
320 ibid 319–25.
321 ibid 320.
322 ibid; however, there seems to be some inconsistency on this point, cf ibid 321–35, where just 36 criminal proceedings are reported.
323 ibid 321–35, especially, claims nos 15, 134, 178, 190, 269, 288, 306.
324 Osservatorio sulla Responsabilità Medica (OR.Me.), 'Osservatorio Orme: la responsabilità sanitaria, problemi e prospettive', *Sanità24* (23 March 2015) <www.sanita24.ilsole24ore.com/art/commenti/2015-03-23/responsabilita-sanitaria-problemi-prospettive-111614.php?uuid=AbI2JEWL> accessed 8 June 2023.
325 Corrado Cartoni, 'Il giudice civile e la responsabilità sanitaria' (2013) Giust Civ 531, 542.

experts' testimonies in around 87% of cases;[326] and, as regards distribution of the decisions over time, there were 82 decisions in 2001, which number increased to 350 in 2003 and peaked at 363 in 2005 before decreasing to 236 in 2007.[327]

Subsequently, medico-legal researchers accessed the archives of the very same civil court and found that from 2001 to 2015 there were 4,386 medical litigation cases.[328]

A very recent study has shown that from 2000 to 2015 there were 4,793 criminal proceedings concerning medical malpractice.[329]

As regards the *Cassazione*, a book reporting the full text of many civil and criminal decisions on medical malpractice issued by that court from 1961 to 1999 has been published,[330] though it is not easy to say whether it contains all the cases decided by that court or just a sample, as few details on the methods are given.[331]

Italian Regions are relevant and perhaps partially unexplored sources of data.

For instance, the Directorate General of *Regione Lombardia*, together with an insurance broker, publishes the risk mapping of its healthcare system, including information about all its hospitals since 1999.[332] During the first decade of the XXI century, more and more Italian Regions implemented systems for monitoring medical malpractice claims, and in 2009 a national program for monitoring errors in healthcare delivery was put in place.[333] Researchers have stated that data from Lombardia and Piemonte reveals that as of 31 December 2009 around 26% of claims against their hospitals had been abandoned, but 92% of those that had been closed resulted in payment.[334] However, the most recent Lombardia report states that as of 31 December 2020 around 42% of claims filed between 1999 and 2009 have been abandoned, around 45% have been paid, and the

---

326 ibid 543.

327 ibid 542.

328 Roberto Manca, Valerio Bruti, Simona Napoletano and Enrico Marinelli, 'A 15 Years Survey for Dental Malpractice Claims in Rome, Italy' (2018) 58 J Forensic Leg Med 74.

329 Camilla Bernardinangeli, Carolina Giannace, Simone Cerciello, Vincenzo M Grassi, Maria Lodise, Giuseppe Vetrugno and Fabio De-Giorgio, 'A Fifteen-Year Survey for Orthopedic Malpractice Claims in the Criminal Court of Rome' (2023) 11 Healthcare 962.

330 Angelo Fiori, Enrico Bottone and Enrico D'Alessandro, *Quarant'anni di giurisprudenza della cassazione nella responsabilità medica* (Giuffrè 2000).

331 Some scholars, when referring to that book, describe it as a report of all the decisions on medical malpractice issued during that period by the *Corte di cassazione*, see Izzo and Pascuzzi (n 314) 30 fn 2; however, other researchers have subsequently stated that they verified and enlarged the data set of the very same book with other sources, see Grembi and Garoupa (n 313) 432, which suggests that some cases may have not been reported in the book.

332 Regione Lombardia and Aon S.p.A. Insurance & Reinsurance Brokers (n 299).

333 Amaral-Garcia and Grembi, 'Curb Your Premium: The Impact of Monitoring Malpractice Claims' (n 271) 140–41.

334 Amaral-Garcia and Grembi, 'Economia della malpractice medica' (n 271) 29–31.

rest are still open.[335] Between 2004 and 2008, the public healthcare facilities in Emilia-Romagna had 6,065 claims (consistently around 1,500 per year),[336] 4,393 (72.43%) of which were exclusively extra-judicial requests for compensation; of these, 1,535 were closed within that period: 853 with a payment (54.46%), 524 rejected by the hospital or its insurer (34.14%) and 175 (11.40%) abandoned. The Regione Emilia-Romagna report recognises that multiple scenarios are possible. For instance, an extra-judicial request can be followed by a civil trial, but claims can also originate from criminal proceedings, and it is possible to have parallel criminal and civil proceedings, as well as submit a claim for damages in a criminal trial. Consequently, for the 2004–08 period, the report considers with great accuracy 6,757 different paths deriving from the aforementioned 6,065 claims. Specifically, it notes 546 (9%) civil trials, 84.61% of which (n=462) concurred with an extra-judicial request for compensation and 1% were sided by related criminal proceedings. Additionally, it is stated that 50 civil trials concluded during this period, of which 40 with a settlement agreement, two with a judgment for claimant and eight with a judgment for defendant, either for lack of negligence (seven cases) or because the action was time-barred (one case).[337]

The evidence is mixed on defensive medicine in Italy before the age of reforms.

On the one hand, Italian doctors stated in several surveys that they practice defensive medicine. According to a 2007 article, 33.4% of the 304 interviewed radiologists and radiotherapists reported to have been asked to pay damages either in a civil controversy or in a criminal trial at some time in their career, and of these 39% admitted that they changed their behaviour afterwards.[338] In 2008, around 300 doctors responded to a survey administered by the *Centro Studi Federico Stella sulla Giustizia penale e la Politica criminale* (Federico Stella Centre on Criminal Justice and Policy) at the *Università Cattolica del Sacro Cuore*, sponsored by the *Società Italiana di Chirurgia* (Italian Surgery Society), 77.9% of which admitted to practicing defensive medicine at least once during the last month of work, including prescribing unnecessary laboratory tests (61.3%) and/or unnecessary consultations with other specialists (58.6%), requiring unnecessary hospitalisation (69.8%). 80.4% of the clinicians additionally stated that their behaviour was prompted by fear of criminal

335 Regione Lombardia and Aon S.p.A. Insurance & Reinsurance Brokers (n 299) 79.

336 Regione Emilia-Romagna (n 298) 11.

337 ibid 41–43.

338 Adriano Fileni, Nicola Magnavita, Francesca Mammi, Giovanni Mandoliti, Francesco Lucà, Giulia Magnavita and Andrea Bergamaschi, 'Malpractice Stress Syndrome in Radiologists and Radiotherapists: Perceived Causes and Consequences' (2007) 112 Radiol Med 1069, 1072–73.

prosecution.[339] In a survey within the Academy of Emergency Medicine and Care of 2011, 90.5% of the around 1,300 interviewed doctors from different specialties stated to have practiced defensive medicine at least once during the last month of work, including prescribing unnecessary laboratory tests (77.7%) and/or unnecessary consultations with other specialists (67.3%) and/or requiring unnecessary hospitalisation to accommodate requests by the patient's family (63.3%).[340] And further examples of this kind of research can be found.[341]

On the other hand, the perception by Italian practitioners of the defensive medicine problem seems inconsistent with the limited data gathered on their actual activity. In 2000, a survey on obstetricians working in public hospitals in Puglia reported that doctors working in units with high caesarean section rates stated to have changed their behaviour due to the risk of malpractice claims.[342] But a study showed some years later that the introduction of experience-rated premiums in Piemonte, which involve higher malpractice liability pressure, surprisingly decreased the average incidence of caesarean sections, without negative impacts on patients.[343] However, experimental research performed by other scholars recently showed that introducing malpractice liability pressure leads physicians to choose a higher amount of medical services.[344]

Conclusions

The first part of this chapter was aimed at depicting the features of the legal and institutional landscape of medical malpractice in France, Germany and Italy before the age of the reforms.

339 Maurizio Catino, 'Blame Culture and Defensive Medicine' (2009) 11 Cogn Tech Work 245, 249–50; Gabrio Forti, Maurizio Catino, Francesco D'Alessandro, Claudia Mazzuccato and Gianluca Varraso (eds), *Il problema della medicina difensiva* (Edizioni ETS 2010) 30–31, 35–36, 39–40; 249–50.

340 Maurizio Catino, Massimo Pesenti Campagnoni and Chiara Locatelli, 'La medicina difensiva: una ricerca sul Pronto Soccorso in Italia' (2011) 5 Pratica Medica & Aspetti Legali 35.

341 Luca Elli, Andrea Tenca, Marco Soncini, Giancarlo Spinzi, Elisabetta Buscarini and Dario Conte, 'Defensive Medicine Practices among Gastroenterologists in Lombardy: Between Lawsuits and the Economic Crisis' (2013) 45 Dig Liver Dis 469; Sergio Motta, Domenico Testa, Ugo Cesari, Giuseppe Quaremba and Gaetano Motta, 'Medical Liability, Defensive Medicine and Professional Insurance in Otolaryngology' (2015) 8 BMC Res Notes 343.

342 Antonella Vimercati, Pantaleo Greco, Anila Kardashi, Cristina Rossi, Vera Loizzi, Marco Scioscia and Giuseppe Loverro, 'Choice of Cesarean Section and Perception of Legal Pressure' (2000) 28 J Perinat Med 111, 114.

343 Sofia Amaral-Garcia, Paola Bertoli and Veronica Grembi, 'Does Experience Rating Improve Obstetric Practices? Evidence from Italy' (2015) 24 Health Econ 1050, 1062–63.

344 Massimo Finocchiaro Castroa, Paolo Lorenzo Ferrara, Calogero Guccio and Domenico Lisi, 'Medical Malpractice Liability and Physicians' Behavior: Experimental Evidence' (2019) 166 J Econ Behav Organ 646.

From a legal perspective, the rules of liability have been investigated, distinguishing between the role of criminal liability, which is ancillary, and that of civil liability, which is the protagonist of the increase in litigation observed at the end of the XX century for each of the earlier analysed systems. In this context, legal standards are inherently complex, but their aims always swing between compensation, which occasionally comes close to indemnifying anyone who has been the likely victim of a medical error, and deterrence, ie to induce healthcare providers, and especially hospitals, to perform their activities in a safer way.

From the institutional perspective, the procedural aspects have been analysed, which sometimes appeared inconsistent with the substantive law of the time. This is largely due to the latent nature of the rules of liability, which derive mostly from case law also in these Civil Law systems. The procedural solutions seem to have had the sole aim of rapidly resolving controversies. This was pursued, for instance, through the use of alternative dispute resolution systems, which act as floodgate-keeping mechanisms for litigation, bringing controversies out of the complex doctrinal and jurisdictional elaboration of the liability rules, albeit with the risk of creating a sort of parallel *Kadi* justice systems.[345]

The second part of this chapter, referring to the available statistical data, is necessarily probabilistic, given the lack of homogeneous data. Therefore, this information is intended only to support the assessment of the sustainability of the earlier analysed legal systems. From this perspective, one notices that the soaring costs of claims are paired with lower availability of insurance, which might prevent the full achievement of the compensatory objective of medical malpractice law. Also, since evidence of an improvement in healthcare deriving from the fear of litigation is almost absent or mixed, one deduces that the deterrent effect has failed to materialise either. Evidence of defensive medicine too is almost absent or mixed, and while it might complicate matters for claimants' lawyers, it does not lead to better medical treatments.

As said, empirical data is aimed only at illustrating which systems appear sustainable, ie in an acceptable balance between different but essential aims and between benefits and costs, and therefore not requiring radical reform, and which systems instead seemed to face an unsustainable imbalance.

It has also to be pointed out that the factors potentially influencing a system's equilibrium are not limited to liability rules, especially if these are conceived in the light of abstract justice theories.

---

345 Max Weber, *Economy and Society: An Outline of Interpretive Sociology*, vol 2 (Guenther Roth and Claus Wittich eds, UC Press, 1978) 814, 892.

Accordingly, it seems that the overall picture exhibits signs of imbalance in each of the countries considered.

Around the end of the XX century, France, Germany and Italy all experienced a surge in medical malpractice litigation.

In France, the 1980s witnessed a decrease in frequency of requests for compensation against clinicians while claims against hospitals in the Paris area slightly increased. At the beginning of the 1990s, more of these claims reached the courts. Between 1990 and 2002, the number of civil trials and interim procedures on medical malpractice at the *tribunaux de grande instance* increased fivefold, and this is much more than the increase in medical activities, which was 20% between 1990 and 2001. Data from the administrative tribunals came later, indicating a slight increase at around the beginning of the XXI century.

In Germany, the number of applications submitted to the *Gutachterkommissionen* and the *Schlichtungsstellen* has been almost always increasing: the rise was very steady in West Germany before reunification (+149% between 1981 and 1991) and slowed during the following decades (+71% between 1992 and 2002; +12% between 2002 and 2012). From 1999 to 2012, the number of opinions issued by the MDK rose by approximately 29%. The number of medical malpractice cases decided by German courts between 2004 and 2012 registered a growth of 34%.

As regards Italy, ANIA estimates that claims more than trebled in five years between 1994 and 2000, and then decreased slightly during the first decade of the XXI century. Multiple sources report the number of Italian lawsuits increased in the 1980s and 1990s.

Concerning liability insurance, the average cost to settle medical malpractice claims in France rose by around 50% in the 1990s, following a path that seems different from that of other liability sectors.

Immediately before the reforms, the German and Italian insurance markets were flawed.

The number of claims filed with insurance companies against German doctors decreased at the beginning of the XXI century, but the liability insurance sector became unprofitable for the carriers (which lamented an unexpected increase in the costs of claims and required higher premiums from both doctors and hospitals), while some companies left the market.

In Italy, the same sector was unprofitable for years, especially with regard to hospital liability insurance, and again this seems different from other liability sectors. Thus, Italian companies left the medical liability market, substituted by foreign carriers. Still, obtaining insurance was challenging for hospitals; in 2008, the average premium for most facilities had increased more than twofold since 2001. Accordingly, there has been a massive shift towards risk retention systems, or at least towards policies with considerable self-insured retention clauses.

Suggested Further Reading List

Hondius E (ed), *The Development of Medical Liability* (CUP 2010)

Koch B E (ed), *Medical Liability in Europe: A Comparison of Selected Jurisdictions* (De Gruyter 2011)

Oliphant K and Wright R W (eds), *Medical Malpractice and Compensation in Global Perspective* (De Gruyter 2013)

Stauch M, *The Law of Medical Negligence in England and in Germany: A Comparative Analysis* (Hart 2008)

Taylor S, *Medical Accident Liability and Redress in English and French Law* (CUP 2015)

2 The Age of Medical Malpractice Statutes
What Has Been Targeted?

France

Since the 1960s, French scholars have proposed the adoption of a no-fault compensation scheme for medical malpractice.[1] Subsequently, several reform projects were drafted from that perspective.[2] However, by the end of the XX century, the legislature had adopted similar arrangements only for limited sectors, such as vaccinations, blood transfusions and experimental therapeutics,[3] while insurers[4] and doctors[5] lobbied for a general no-fault compensation approach.

The limited success of no-fault compensation schemes has not closed the debate on medical malpractice reforms in France. In accordance with the constitutional setting adopted for the Fifth Republic, the most important phase of the debate (although not the only one), takes place in commissions established by the relevant ministries to study reforms. Thus, reports on medical malpractice have also been commissioned. For instance, in 1980, the Mac Aleese commission established by the Ministry of Justice suggested, among other things, to separate civil actions from criminal trials, to exclude claims for damages from the administrative jurisdiction, to shorten the limitation periods and to promote alternative dispute resolution systems.[6] This last suggestion was the only one taken up by the government, albeit unsuccessfully.[7]

---

1 Jean Penneau, 'La réforme de la responsabilité médicale: responsabilité ou assurance' (1990) 42 Rev Intern Dr Comp 525, 542–44.
2 François Ewald and Henri Margeat, 'Le risque thérapeutique' (1991) 6 Risques 9, 27ff <www.revue-risques.fr/wp-content/uploads/Risques-006_Web.pdf> accessed 4 July 2023.
3 Sophie Gromb, 'Responsabilité médicale: va-t-on indemniser l'accident mèdical?' (1996) 16 Médecine & Droit 12, 15.
4 Christian Sicot, 'Responsabilité médicale: l'expérience du groupe des assurances mutuelles médicales (GAMM)' (1998) 182 Bulletin de l'Académie nationale de médecine 542.
5 Pierre Vayre, 'Le risque aléatoire en chirurgie et l'indemnisation de son préjudice en procédure civile' (1998) 123 Chirurgie (Paris) 206.
6 Penneau (n 1) 539–41.
7 ibid. Later on, see *Ordonnance no 96–346 du 24 avril 1996 portant réforme de l'hospitalisation publique et privée*, art 1.

DOI: 10.4324/9781003440277-3

The first relevant legislative amendment in France regarded the field of criminal law. The principle of the identity of civil and criminal negligence, established by case law, was abandoned after *loi n° 2000–647 du 10 juillet 2000 tendant à préciser la définition des délits non intentionnels.*[8] This act modified art 121–3 of the Criminal Code on the general requirements for negligent crimes, making them more difficult to meet when the defendant has indirectly contributed to the harm,[9] and art 4–1 of the Code of Criminal Procedure, allowing civil trial for damages when the criminal law requirements cannot be met.[10]

After a couple of years, *loi n°2002–303 du 4 mars 2002 relative aux droits des malades et à la qualité du système de santé*, the so-called *loi Kouchner*,

---

8   Jean Penneau, 'Médecine – Médecins', *Répertoire de droit pénal et de procédure pénale* (Octobre 2010) (actualisation: Juin 2022) para 82 <www-dalloz-fr> accessed 28 August 2023; Elisabeth Fortis, 'La nouvelle définition des délits non intentionnels par la loi du 10 juillet 2000' (2001) RSC 737.

9   'Il y a également délit, lorsque la loi le prévoit, en cas de faute d'imprudence, de négligence ou de manquement à une obligation de prudence ou de sécurité prévue par la loi ou le règlement, s'il est établi que l'auteur des faits n'a pas accompli les diligences normales compte tenu, le cas échéant, de la nature de ses missions ou de ses fonctions, de ses compétences ainsi que du pouvoir et des moyens dont il disposait.

   Dans le cas prévu par l'alinéa qui précède, les personnes physiques qui n'ont pas causé directement le dommage, mais qui ont créé ou contribué à créer la situation qui a permis la réalisation du dommage ou qui n'ont pas pris les mesures permettant de l'éviter, sont responsables pénalement s'il est établi qu'elles ont, soit violé de façon manifestement délibérée une obligation particulière de prudence ou de sécurité prévue par la loi ou le règlement, soit commis une faute caractérisée et qui exposait autrui à un risque d'une particulière gravité qu'elles ne pouvaient ignorer'.

   See also the current formulation of C pén, art 221–6 (*version en vigueur depuis le 19 mai 2011*): 'Le fait de causer, dans les conditions et selon les distinctions prévues à l'article 121–3, par maladresse, imprudence, inattention, négligence ou manquement à une obligation de prudence ou de sécurité imposée par la loi ou le règlement, la mort d'autrui constitue un homicide involontaire puni de trois ans d'emprisonnement et de 45 000 euros d'amende.

   En cas de violation manifestement délibérée d'une obligation particulière de prudence ou de sécurité imposée par la loi ou le règlement, les peines encourues sont portées à cinq ans d'emprisonnement et à 75 000 euros d'amende'.

   And finally, see the current formulation of C pén, art 221–19 (*Version en vigueur depuis le 19 mai 2011*): 'Le fait de causer à autrui, dans les conditions et selon les distinctions prévues à l'article 121–3, par maladresse, imprudence, inattention, négligence ou manquement à une obligation de prudence ou de sécurité imposée par la loi ou le règlement, une incapacité totale de travail pendant plus de trois mois est puni de deux ans d'emprisonnement et de 30 000 euros d'amende.

   En cas de violation manifestement délibérée d'une obligation particulière de prudence ou de sécurité imposée par la loi ou le règlement, les peines encourues sont portées à trois ans d'emprisonnement et à 45 000 euros d'amende'.

10 'L'absence de faute pénale non intentionnelle au sens de l'article 121–3 du code pénal ne fait pas obstacle à l'exercice d'une action devant les juridictions civiles afin d'obtenir la réparation d'un dommage sur le fondement de l'article 1383 du code civil si l'existence de la faute civile prévue par cet article est établie ou en application de l'article L. 452–1 du code de la sécurité sociale si l'existence de la faute inexcusable prévue par cet article est établie'.

entered into force. On the one hand, this act is related to specific and much debated cases. For instance, it repealed the case law on wrongful life stemming from the *affaire Perruche*.[11] On the other hand, the drafters also took the opportunity to address more general issues of medical malpractice law. For instance, the legislature was well aware of the separate limitation regimes of administrative and private law, as well as their conflicting treatment of *aléa thérapeutique*,[12] for which the government wanted to put in place a no-fault compensation scheme, estimating a cost of between 1 and 1.5 billion francs.[13]

Thus, besides strict liability for nosocomial infections and for defective medical products, the reform reaffirmed the general rule of liability by fault, irrespective of the entitlement relied on by the claimant and of the jurisdiction. The *loi Kouchner* also imposed a duty on doctors and hospitals to inform the victim on the circumstances and the causes of iatrogenic injuries.[14] In cases where the liability of the healthcare providers could not be proved, a '*réparation des préjudices du patient au titre de la solidarité nationale*' (ie a no-fault compensation scheme) was set up to cover those accidents directly

---

11 Cass ass plén 17 novembre 2000, D 2001, 332.

    Loi Kouchner (version initiale), art 1: 'I. – Nul ne peut se prévaloir d'un préjudice du seul fait de sa naissance.

    La personne née avec un handicap dû à une faute médicale peut obtenir la réparation de son préjudice lorsque l'acte fautif a provoqué directement le handicap ou l'a aggravé, ou n'a pas permis de prendre les mesures susceptibles de l'atténuer.

    Lorsque la responsabilité d'un professionnel ou d'un établissement de santé est engagée vis-à-vis des parents d'un enfant né avec un handicap non décelé pendant la grossesse à la suite d'une faute caractérisée, les parents peuvent demander une indemnité au titre de leur seul préjudice. Ce préjudice ne saurait inclure les charges particulières découlant, tout au long de la vie de l'enfant, de ce handicap. La compensation de ce dernier relève de la solidarité nationale'.

    Nowadays, see *Code de l'action sociale et des familles* (Social Action and Family Code), art L114–5.

12 Claude Evin, Bernard Charles and Jean-Jacques Denis, *Rapport d'information de MM. Claude Evin, Bernard Charles et Jean-Jacques Denis, déposé en application de l'article 145 du règlement par la commission des affaires culturelles, sur la loi n° 2002–303 du 4 mars 2002 relative aux droits des malades et à la qualité du système de santé (n° 3688, 11 avril 2002)* <www.assemblee-nationale.fr/11/rap-info/i3688.asp> accessed 28 August 2023.

13 *Audition de M. Bernard Kouchner, ministre délégué à la santé, sur le projet de loi relatif aux droits des malades et la qualité du système de santé – n° 3258 (MM. Claude Evin, Jean-Jacques Denis, Bernard Charles, rapporteurs)* <www.assemblee-nationale.fr/11/cr-cafc/00-01/c0001049.asp> accessed 28 August 2023.

14 *Loi Kouchner (version initiale)*, art 98, which introduced *code de la santé publique* (CSP) (public health code), art L 1142–4: 'Toute personne victime ou s'estimant victime d'un dommage imputable à une activité de prévention, de diagnostic ou de soins ou ses ayants droit, si la personne est décédée, ou, le cas échéant, son représentant légal, doit être informée par le professionnel, l'établissement de santé, les services de santé ou l'organisme concerné sur les circonstances et les causes de ce dommage.

    Cette information lui est délivrée au plus tard dans les quinze jours suivant la découverte du dommage ou sa demande expresse, lors d'un entretien au cours duquel la personne peut se faire assister par un médecin ou une autre personne de son choix'.

attributable to preventive, diagnostic or therapeutic acts having abnormal consequences and of serious nature (eg resulting in a permanent incapacity rate of more than 24% to the patient).[15] The scheme was to be administered by the *Office national d'indemnisation des accidents médicaux, des affections iatrogènes et des infections nosocomiales* (ONIAM) (National Office for Compensation of Medical Accidents, Iatrogenic Diseases and Nosocomial Infections), financed mainly by the health insurance funds.[16]

15 *Loi Kouchner* (version initiale), art 98 inserted CSP, art L 1142–1: 'I. – Hors le cas où leur responsabilité est encourue en raison d'un défaut d'un produit de santé, les professionnels de santé mentionnés à la quatrième partie du présent code, ainsi que tout établissement, service ou organisme dans lesquels sont réalisés des actes individuels de prévention, de diagnostic ou de soins ne sont responsables des conséquences dommageables d'actes de prévention, de diagnostic ou de soins qu'en cas de faute.

Les établissements, services et organismes susmentionnés sont responsables des dommages résultant d'infections nosocomiales, sauf s'ils rapportent la preuve d'une cause étrangère.

II. – Lorsque la responsabilité d'un professionnel, d'un établissement, service ou organisme mentionné au I ou d'un producteur de produits n'est pas engagée, un accident médical, une affection iatrogène ou une infection nosocomiale ouvre droit à la réparation des préjudices du patient au titre de la solidarité nationale, lorsqu'ils sont directement imputables à des actes de prévention, de diagnostic ou de soins et qu'ils ont eu pour le patient des conséquences anormales au regard de son état de santé comme de l'évolution prévisible de celui-ci et présentent un caractère de gravité, fixé par décret, apprécié au regard de la perte de capacités fonctionnelles et des conséquences sur la vie privée et professionnelle mesurées en tenant notamment compte du taux d'incapacité permanente ou de la durée de l'incapacité temporaire de travail.

Ouvre droit à réparation des préjudices au titre de la solidarité nationale un taux d'incapacité permanente supérieur à un pourcentage d'un barème spécifique fixé par décret; ce pourcentage, au plus égal à 25 %, est déterminé par ledit décret'.

The requirements for accessing the no-fault scheme have been slightly amended by *loi n°2009–526 du 12 mai 2009*, art 112, which refers to the 'taux d'atteinte permanente à l'intégrité physique ou psychique, de la durée de l'arrêt temporaire des activités professionnelles ou de celle du déficit fonctionnel temporaire' ('the rate of permanent harm to the physical or mental integrity, the duration of the temporary suspensions of professional activities or the duration of the temporary functional deficit').

See also CSP, art D 1142–1: 'Le pourcentage mentionné au dernier alinéa de l'article L. 1142–1 est fixé à 24 %.

Présente également le caractère de gravité mentionné au II de l'article L. 1142–1 un accident médical, une affection iatrogène ou une infection nosocomiale ayant entraîné, pendant une durée au moins égale à six mois consécutifs ou à six mois non consécutifs sur une période de douze mois, un arrêt temporaire des activités professionnelles ou des gênes temporaires constitutives d'un déficit fonctionnel temporaire supérieur ou égal à un taux de 50 %.

A titre exceptionnel, le caractère de gravité peut être reconnu:

1° Lorsque la victime est déclarée définitivement inapte à exercer l'activité professionnelle qu'elle exerçait avant la survenue de l'accident médical, de l'affection iatrogène ou de l'infection nosocomiale;

2° Ou lorsque l'accident médical, l'affection iatrogène ou l'infection nosocomiale occasionne des troubles particulièrement graves, y compris d'ordre économique, dans ses conditions d'existence'.

On the requirement of a serious harm, see also Simon Taylor, *Medical Accident Liability and Redress in English and French Law* (CUP 2015) 102–04.

16 *Loi Kouchner* (version initiale), art 98, which introduced CSP, arts L 1142–22ff.

The same act has also established a uniform 10-year limitation period '*à compter de la consolidation du dommage*' ('starting from the date of consolidation of the injury'), the duration of which is thus independent of whether the case is based on contract, tort or administrative law.[17] However, reference to the consolidation of the injury as a starting point for the limitation period makes claims *de facto* imprescriptible.[18]

In 2008, the French legislature introduced a general *délai butoir* (long-stop) of 20 years under art 2232 *Code civil*, but this does not apply to liability for bodily injuries.[19] Interestingly, however, medical malpractice cases were expressly excluded from the scope of the said long-stop by another specific provision,[20] which was repealed in 2016.[21] Anyways, this 20-year period runs '*à compter du jour de la naissance du droit*' ('from the day on which the right arose'), which in medical malpractice cases coincides with the time of

---

17 *Loi Kouchner* (version initiale), art 98 introduced CSP, art L 1142–28: 'Les actions tendant à mettre en cause la responsabilité des professionnels de santé ou des établissements de santé publics ou privés à l'occasion d'actes de prévention, de diagnostic ou de soins se prescrivent par dix ans à compter de la consolidation du dommage'; Emmanuel Terrier and Jean Penneau, 'Médecine: réparation des conséquences des risques sanitaires', *Répertoire de droit civil Dalloz* (Octobre 2020) (actualisation: Mars 2023) paras 15 and 354 <www-dalloz-fr> accessed 29 August 2023; however, other aspects of the statute of limitations required further legislative interventions in order to unify the administrative and private law regimes, see Caroline Grossholz, 'Hôpitaux: régimes de responsabilité et de solidarité', *Répertoire de la responsabilité de la puissance publique Dalloz* (Février 2018) (actualisation: Février 2023) paras 45–47 <www-dalloz-fr> accessed 29 August 2023.

18 Jean-Sébastien Borghetti, 'France', in Israel Gilead and Bjarte Askeland (eds), *Prescription in Tort Law: Analytical and Comparative Perspectives* (Intersentia 2020) 326.

19 *Loi n°2008–561 du 17 juin 2008*, art 1 introduced C civ, art 2232 (*version en vigueur du 19 juin 2008 au 10 août 2016*): 'Le report du point de départ, la suspension ou l'interruption de la prescription ne peut avoir pour effet de porter le délai de la prescription extinctive au-delà de vingt ans à compter du jour de la naissance du droit.

Le premier alinéa n'est pas applicable dans les cas mentionnés aux articles 2226, 2227, 2233 et 2236, au premier alinéa de l'article 2241 et à l'article 2244. Il ne s'applique pas non plus aux actions relatives à l'état des personnes'.

20 *Loi n°2008–561 du 17 juin 2008*, art 20, which introduced CSP, art L1142–28 al 2: 'Ces actions ne sont pas soumises au délai mentionné à l'article 2232 du code civil'.

21 *Loi n° 2016–41 du 26 janvier 2016 de modernisation de notre système de santé*, art 188; Commission des Affaires Sociales, *Rapport fait au nom de la Commission des Affaires Sociales sur le projet de loi relatif à la santé, par m. Olivier Véran, mme Bernadette Laclais, m. Jean-Louis Touraine, mme Hélène Geoffroy et m. Richard Ferrand* <www.assemblee-nationale.fr/14/rapports/r2673.asp> accessed 15 September 2023: 'Le second alinéa de l'article L. 1142–28 exclut l'application de l'article 2232 du code civil aux actions en responsabilité médicale. Celui-ci dispose que, dans la généralité des cas, «le report du point de départ, la suspension ou l'interruption de la prescription ne peut avoir pour effet de porter le délai de la prescription extinctive au-delà de vingt ans à compter du jour de la naissance du droit». Cet alinéa est réécrit par le I de l'article 45 ter, qui prévoit au cas d'espèce l'application des dispositions du titre XX du livre III du code civil (« De la prescription extinctive»), à l'exclusion de celles de son chapitre II («Des délais et du point de départ de la prescription extinctive»). Cela aura notamment pour conséquence de rendre désormais applicable l'article 2232'.

consolidation of the harm, making the long-stop of little practical significance in this area.

The *loi Kouchner* made insurance mandatory for healthcare providers and stipulated that hospitals' policies must cover the professionals they employ.[22] If a carrier refused twice to underwrite the liability of a healthcare provider, the provider could request a *'bureau central de tarification'* ('central pricing office') to set the premium, in consideration of which the company was then obliged to underwrite.[23]

Moreover, new *'commissions régionales de conciliation et d'indemnisation des accidents médicaux'* (regional conciliation and compensation commissions) were set up to provide for an optional system of out-of-court settlement of disputes for serious fault and no-fault cases.[24] If the regional commission found the healthcare provider liable, its insurer or the ONIAM would offer compensation to the victim, who could then settle the case through acceptance thereof.[25] The *Commission nationale des accidents médicaux* (CNAMed) (national commission on medical accidents) was established to ensure that the rules are applied consistently by the regional commissions.[26]

Concerned that the *loi Kouchner* might make it more difficult for healthcare providers to obtain insurance,[27] the legislature adopted some modifications vis-à-vis *loi n°2002–1577 du 30 décembre 2002 relative à la responsabilité civile médicale*, the so-called *loi About*. In particular, the state took over the compensation of nosocomial infections causing a permanent disability rate of more than 25% or death.[28] Moreover, the government was allowed to authorise, on a case-by-case basis, public hospitals to establish risk retention systems instead of taking out insurance,[29] which as of today has been granted only to the *Assistance Publique* (ie the public body entrusted with healthcare in the Paris area).[30] Pursuant to *loi About*, claims made and extension clauses became mandatory for medical and hospital liability policies.[31]

After almost a decade, a *fonds de garantie* (ie a supplementary compensation fund) financed by annual contributions from independent practitioners

---

22 *Loi Kouchner* (version initiale), art 98 introduced CSP, art. L 1142–2; see also *loi Kouchner* (version initiale), art 100, which introduced *Code des assurances* (C assur) (Insurance Code), art L 251–1.
23 *Loi Kouchner* (version initiale), art 100, which introduced C assur, arts L 252–1 and L 252–2.
24 *Loi Kouchner* (version initiale), art 98, which introduced CSP, arts L 1142–4ff.
25 ibid arts L 1142–14ff.
26 *Loi Kouchner* (version initiale), art 92, which introduced CSP, art L1142–10.
27 *Proposition de loi de M. Nicolas ABOUT relative à la responsabilité civile médicale, n° 33 (2002–2003)* <www.senat.fr/leg/ppl02-033.html> accessed 30 August 2023.
28 *Loi About*, art 1.
29 ibid.
30 Lydia Velliscig, *Assicurazione e "autoassicurazione" nella gestione dei rischi sanitari. Studio di diritto comparato* (Giuffrè 2018) 239–40.
31 *Loi About*, art 4 introduced C assur, art L 251–2.

was established for those cases in which their policies could not operate due to, for example, ceilings.[32]

Finally, the procedural and evidence rules relating to medical malpractice trials have not undergone significant changes in France.

Germany

The doctrinal debate on the reform of medical malpractice law in West Germany dates to the 1960s and reached its peak in 1978, when the proposal to introduce a comprehensive no-fault compensation scheme was rejected by the majority of participants.[33] Notably, such a scheme was adopted in East Germany and then repealed after the reunification.[34]

In 2001 and 2002, almost at the same time as the French medical malpractice reforms, Germany adopted some new general private law provisions that also applied to the liability of healthcare providers, which in turn was addressed by a specific statute just a decade later.

On the acts concerning general private law, the *Schuldrechtsmodernisierungsgesetz* (act for the modernisation of the law of obligations)[35] standardised the limitation period for all claims for damages arising from negligent bodily injuries to 30 years from the date on which the act, breach of duty or other event that caused the injury occurred, irrespective of the contractual or tortious nature of the claim.[36] In addition, the *Zweites Schadensersatzrechtsänderungsgesetz* (second act for the amendment of the law of damages)[37] allowed compensation for bodily injuries also in contractual claims.[38]

In 2013, the *Patientenrechtegesetz* (patients' rights act)[39] introduced the new §§ 630a–630h into the BGB, addressing medical malpractice. This reform primarily sought to codify the solutions already found in case law in

---

32 See *loi n° 2011-1977 du 28 décembre 2011*, which introduced C assur, art L. 426–1.

33 Marc Stauch, *The Law of Medical Negligence in England and in Germany: A Comparative Analysis* (Hart 2008) 144–45.

34 ibid 145–46.

35 *Gesetz zur Modernisierung des Schuldrechts vom 26. November 2001 (BGBl I S 3138).*

36 § 199(2) BGB: 'Schadensersatzansprüche, die auf der Verletzung des Lebens, des Körpers, der Gesundheit oder der Freiheit beruhen, verjähren ohne Rücksicht auf ihre Entstehung und die Kenntnis oder grob fahrlässige Unkenntnis in 30 Jahren von der Begehung der Handlung, der Pflichtverletzung oder dem sonstigen, den Schaden auslösenden Ereignis an'.

37 *Zweites Gesetz zur Änderung schadensersatzrechtlicher Vorschriften vom 19. Juli 2002 (BGBl I S 2674).*

38 § 253 BGB: '(1) Wegen eines Schadens, der nicht Vermögensschaden ist, kann Entschädigung in Geld nur in den durch das Gesetz bestimmten Fällen gefordert werden.

(2) Ist wegen einer Verletzung des Körpers, der Gesundheit, der Freiheit oder der sexuellen Selbstbestimmung Schadensersatz zu leisten, kann auch wegen des Schadens, der nicht Vermögensschaden ist, eine billige Entschädigung in Geld gefordert werden'.

39 *Gesetz zur Verbesserung der Rechte von Patientinnen und Patienten vom 20. Februar 2013 (BGBl I S 277).*

order to achieve greater transparency and legal certainty for the victims of medical malpractice.[40]

This act therefore refers to the *Behandlungsvertrag* (treatment contract), which must be performed according to the generally accepted standards of medical care applicable at the time of treatment, unless otherwise agreed.[41] However, patients can sue healthcare providers also in tort pursuant to § 823 BGB, which makes no distinction as regards the burden of proof,[42] limitations or damages.

§ 630h BGB[43] codifies some rebuttable presumptions in favour of the patient, which had already been recognised by German courts in the past.[44] Thus, if a fully controllable risk of the treatment has materialised,[45] it is presumed that the healthcare provider has made a mistake; if he has failed to enter in

---

40 *Gesetzentwurf der Bundesregierung. Entwurf eines Gesetzes zur Verbesserung der Rechte von Patientinnen und Patienten*, in Deutscher Bundestag, Drucksache 17/10488 of 15 (August 2012) 1 <https://dserver.bundestag.de/btd/17/104/1710488.pdf> accessed 31 August 2023.

41 § 630a BGB: '(1) Durch den Behandlungsvertrag wird derjenige, welcher die medizinische Behandlung eines Patienten zusagt (Behandelnder), zur Leistung der versprochenen Behandlung, der andere Teil (Patient) zur Gewährung der vereinbarten Vergütung verpflichtet, soweit nicht ein Dritter zur Zahlung verpflichtet ist.

(2) Die Behandlung hat nach den zum Zeitpunkt der Behandlung bestehenden, allgemein anerkannten fachlichen Standards zu erfolgen, soweit nicht etwas anderes vereinbart ist'.

42 Erwin Deutsch and Andreas Spickhoff, *Medizinrecht* (7th edn, Springer 2014) 202–03.

43 § 630h BGB: '(1) Ein Fehler des Behandelnden wird vermutet, wenn sich ein allgemeines Behandlungsrisiko verwirklicht hat, das für den Behandelnden voll beherrschbar war und das zur Verletzung des Lebens, des Körpers oder der Gesundheit des Patienten geführt hat.

(2) Der Behandelnde hat zu beweisen, dass er eine Einwilligung gemäß § 630d eingeholt und entsprechend den Anforderungen des § 630e aufgeklärt hat. Genügt die Aufklärung nicht den Anforderungen des § 630e, kann der Behandelnde sich darauf berufen, dass der Patient auch im Fall einer ordnungsgemäßen Aufklärung in die Maßnahme eingewilligt hätte.

(3) Hat der Behandelnde eine medizinisch gebotene wesentliche Maßnahme und ihr Ergebnis entgegen § 630f Absatz 1 oder Absatz 2 nicht in der Patientenakte aufgezeichnet oder hat er die Patientenakte entgegen § 630f Absatz 3 nicht aufbewahrt, wird vermutet, dass er diese Maßnahme nicht getroffen hat.

(4) War ein Behandelnder für die von ihm vorgenommene Behandlung nicht befähigt, wird vermutet, dass die mangelnde Befähigung für den Eintritt der Verletzung des Lebens, des Körpers oder der Gesundheit ursächlich war.

(5) Liegt ein grober Behandlungsfehler vor und ist dieser grundsätzlich geeignet, eine Verletzung des Lebens, des Körpers oder der Gesundheit der tatsächlich eingetretenen Art herbeizuführen, wird vermutet, dass der Behandlungsfehler für diese Verletzung ursächlich war. Dies gilt auch dann, wenn es der Behandelnde unterlassen hat, einen medizinisch gebotenen Befund rechtzeitig zu erheben oder zu sichern, soweit der Befund mit hinreichender Wahrscheinlichkeit ein Ergebnis erbracht hätte, das Anlass zu weiteren Maßnahmen gegeben hätte, und wenn das Unterlassen solcher Maßnahmen grob fehlerhaft gewesen wäre'.

44 Gerhard Wagner, 'BGB § 630h', Rn. 1–3, in Franz Jürgen Säcker, Roland Rixecker, Hartmut Oetker and Bettina Limperg (eds), *Münchener Kommentar zum Bürgerlichen Gesetzbuch* (9th edn, Beck 2023).

45 This essentially refers to organisational shortcomings of the hospital, eg when the patient is insufficiently monitored, see BGH 10.1.1984 – VI ZR 158/82, NJW 1984, 1400, or in instances of defective equipment, see BGH 11.10.1977 – VI ZR 110/75, NJW 1978, 584, or in fall cases, see BGH 18.12.1990 – VI ZR 169/90, NJW 1991, 1540.

the medical record an important treatment or to keep such a record, it is presumed that the treatment has not been carried out; if it turns out that he was not competent to render the treatment provided, it is presumed that his deficiency caused the harm; if a *grober Behandlungsfehler* (gross negligence in the treatment) has been committed,[46] which may have caused the specific harm suffered by the patient, causation is presumed; additionally, the healthcare provider bears the burden of proving that he informed the patient and obtained consent to treatment, or that the patient would have given consent had s/he been properly informed.

The most innovative content of the *Patientenrechtegesetz* is a new duty on doctors to inform the victim on the existence of a recognisable treatment error.[47]

Later, in 2021, a statute made liability insurance mandatory for *Vertragsärzte*, ie physicians performing activities in the ambit of the statutory health insurance funds.[48]

At the procedural level, a reform of the Code of Civil Procedure came into force in 2002, requiring the court to hold a pre-trial conciliation hearing unless another attempt to settle the case had already been made,[49] for example by a *Schlichtungsstelle* of a *Landesaerztekammer* (ie a conciliation commission of a local college of physicians).[50] Another act granted the stay of the proceedings in case the parties access an alternative dispute resolution system following the commencement of legal proceedings.[51]

In 2006[52] and in 2016,[53] minor amendments to the law on expert evidence were adopted in Germany, such as the mandatory setting of a deadline for

---

46 Such as disregarding basic diagnostic and therapeutic rules, eg when after a motor accident the victim lamented pain in walking but her pelvic fracture remained undetected, see BGH, 27.4.2004 – VI ZR 34/03, NJW 2004, 2011, or prescribing a grossly erroneous dosage of a drug, see OLG Köln 7.8.2013–5 U 92/12, JuS 2013, 1130.

47 § 630 c Abs 2 S 2–3 BGB: '²Sind für den Behandelnden Umstände erkennbar, die die Annahme eines Behandlungsfehlers begründen, hat er den Patienten über diese auf Nachfrage oder zur Abwendung gesundheitlicher Gefahren zu informieren. ³Ist dem Behandelnden oder einem seiner in § 52 Absatz 1 der Strafprozessordnung bezeichneten Angehörigen ein Behandlungsfehler unterlaufen, darf die Information nach Satz 2 zu Beweiszwecken in einem gegen den Behandelnden oder gegen seinen Angehörigen geführten Straf- oder Bußgeldverfahren nur mit Zustimmung des Behandelnden verwendet werden'.

48 See *Gesetz zur Weiterentwicklung der Gesundheitsversorgung vom 11. Juli 2021 (BGBl. I 2021 S. 2754)*, which introduced § 95e SGB V.

49 See *Gesetz zur Reform des Zivilprozesses vom 27.07.2001 (BGBl. I S. 1887)*, which modified § 278 ZPO.

50 Deutsch and Spickhoff (n 42) 547–48.

51 See *Gesetz zur Förderung der Mediation und anderer Verfahren der außergerichtlichen Konfliktbeilegung vom 21. Juli 2012 (BGBl. I S. 1577)*, art 1, which introduced § 278a ZPO.

52 *Zweites Gesetz zur Modernisierung der Justiz (2. Justizmodernisierungsgesetz) vom 22. Dezember 2006 (BGBl. I S. 3416)*.

53 *Gesetz zur Änderung des Sachverständigenrechts und zur weiteren Änderung des Gesetzes über das Verfahren in Familiensachen und in den Angelegenheiten der freiwilligen Gerichtsbarkeit sowie zur Änderung des Sozialgerichtsgesetzes, der Verwaltungsgerichtsordnung, der Finanzgerichtsordnung und des Gerichtskostengesetzes vom 11. Oktober 2016 (BGBl. I S. 2222)*.

written report of the court-appointed expert,[54] or the possibility for the judge to order a written explanation or supplement to the report.[55]

Italy

Italian legal scholars have studied foreign no-fault systems, wondering whether a similar solution could be adopted as a reform of Italian medical malpractice law.[56]

In the first decade of the XXI century, enquiry committees set up by Parliament attempted to shed light on the civil liability of hospitals in some Italian Regions.[57]

In 2012, however, the government was the first to take an initiative, adopting a *decreto legge* (ie an order with temporary statutory force)[58] that dealt with civil liability for medical malpractice.[59] Its text seemed to suggest that, in slight negligence cases, compliance with clinical practice guidelines or good medical practices would have shielded health professionals from liability for damages.[60] The reference to clinical practice guidelines

54 § 411(1) ZPO.

55 § 411(3) S 2 ZPO.

56 Giulio Ponzanelli, 'La responsabilità medica ad un bivio: assicurazione obbligatoria, sistema residuale no-fault o risk-management?' (2003) Danno e Resp 428, 430, recalling the French experience; Giovanni Comandé, 'Dalla responsabilità sanitaria al no-blame regionale tra conciliazione e risarcimento' (2010) Danno e Resp 977, 983, mentioning the New Zealand, Scandinavian and Danish examples; Luca Nocco, 'Un no-fault plan come risposta alla "crisi" della responsabilità sanitaria? Uno sguardo sull' "alternativa francese" a dieci anni dalla sua introduzione' (2012) Riv It Med Leg 449; Gianluca Scarchillo, 'La responsabilità medica: risarcimento o indennizzo? Riflessioni, evoluzioni e prospettive di diritto comparato' (2017) Resp Civ Prev 1490, 1502ff, examining the French, Brazilian and Swedish experiences.

57 *Deliberazione 25 luglio 2007 recante Istituzione di una Commissione parlamentare di inchiesta sugli errori in campo sanitario e sulle cause dei disavanzi sanitari regionali, GU 28 luglio 2007 n 174; Deliberazione 5 novembre 2008 recante Istituzione di una Commissione parlamentare di inchiesta sugli errori in campo sanitario e sulle cause dei disavanzi sanitari regionali, GU 20 novembre 2008 n 272.*

58 See art 77 Cost: 'Il Governo non può, senza delegazione delle Camere, emanare decreti che abbiano valore di legge ordinaria.

   Quando, in casi straordinari di necessità e di urgenza, il Governo adotta, sotto la sua responsabilità, provvedimenti provvisori con forza di legge, deve il giorno stesso presentarli per la conversione alle Camere che, anche se sciolte, sono appositamente convocate e si riuniscono entro cinque giorni.

   I decreti perdono efficacia sin dall'inizio, se non sono convertiti in legge entro sessanta giorni dalla loro pubblicazione. Le Camere possono tuttavia regolare con legge i rapporti giuridici sorti sulla base dei decreti non convertiti'.

59 *Decreto legge 13 settembre 2012, n 158 conv con modif in legge 8 novembre 2012, n 189*, the so-called *decreto Balduzzi*.

60 Art 3, co 1 *decreto Balduzzi (in vigore fino all'11 novembre 2012)*: 'Fermo restando il disposto dell'articolo 2236 del codice civile, nell'accertamento della colpa lieve nell'attività dell'esercente le professioni sanitarie il giudice, ai sensi dell'articolo 1176 del codice civile, tiene conto in particolare dell'osservanza, nel caso concreto, delle linee guida e delle buone

was most likely inspired by select statutes previously adopted by certain American states.[61]

Furthermore, the *decreto legge* provided for the application of scheduled damages for bodily injuries in medical malpractice cases, referring to particular provisions of the *Codice delle assicurazioni* (insurance code)[62] applicable to car accidents. Scheduled damages are a specific feature of the Italian experience, allowing a certain degree of standardisation in the calculation of awards for pain and suffering, depending on the age and degree of incapacity of the victim. However, it is worth noting that at the end of 2023, due to a significant delay in the adoption of a regulation by the Italian government, the statutory schedules still only applied to minor bodily injuries,[63] while for major bodily injuries the courts use other schedules that have been jointly elaborated by judges, lawyers, medico-legal experts and scholars.[64]

Just a couple of months after its publication, the *decreto legge* on civil liability for medical malpractice was converted into an act of Parliament,[65] with a very important amendment. The legislature suspected that it could have been unreasonable and unconstitutional to shield practitioners from civil liability while maintaining the risk of criminal liability for the very same conduct.[66] Therefore, the new provision exempted professionals abiding by guidelines

---

pratiche accreditate dalla comunità scientifica nazionale e internazionale'; see also *Disegno di legge di conversione in legge del decreto-legge 13 settembre 2012, n. 158*, 5 <http://documenti. camera.it/_dati/leg16/lavori/stampati/pdf/16PDL0063150.pdf> accessed 1 September 2023.

61 On this legal transplant see Carlo M Masieri, *Linee guida e responsabilità civile del medico. Dall'esperienza americana alla legge Gelli-Bianco* (Giuffrè Francis Lefebvre 2019).

62 Art 3, co 3 *decreto Balduzzi*: 'Il danno biologico conseguente all'attività dell'esercente della professione sanitaria è risarcito sulla base delle tabelle di cui agli articoli 138 e 139 del decreto legislativo 7 settembre 2005, n. 209'.

63 The scheduled damages for *lesioni di lieve entità* (minor bodily injuries), ie up to 9 out 100 points of incapacity, can be inferred by art 139, co 1, lett a and co 6 *Codice delle assicurazioni*; the legislature set 1 May 2022 as the deadline for adopting the regulation regarding bodily injuries causing from 10 to 100 points of incapacity, which unfortunately expired; however, a draft of this regulation has circulated, *Schema di decreto del Presidente della Repubblica – Regolamento recante la tabella delle menomazioni all'integrità psicofisica comprese fra 10 e 100 punti di invalidità, ai sensi dell'articolo 138 del codice delle assicurazioni private di cui al decreto legislativo 7 settembre 2005, n. 209* <https://ridare.it/system/files/articoli/allegati/ Schema%20decreto%20e%20tabelle%20-%20d.P.R.%20su%20138%20MACROLESIONI. pdf> accessed 15 September 2023.

64 Osservatorio sulla Giustizia Civile di Milano, *Tabelle milanesi per la liquidazione del danno non patrimoniale – Edizione 2021* <www.milanosservatorio.it/wp-content/uploads/2021/03/OSS-MI-TABELLE-2021-LIQUIDAZIONE-DANNO-NON-PATRIMONIALE-ALLA-PERSONA. pdf> accessed 15 September 2023; Cass civ sez III 7 giugno 2011 n 12408, in Foro It, 2011, I, 2274.

65 *Legge 8 novembre 2012, n 189*.

66 See *Bollettino delle Giunte e delle Commissioni Parlamentari della Camera dei Deputati – XVI legislatura – Giustizia (II)*, 11 ottobre 2012, 15 <http://documenti.camera.it/leg16/resoconti/ commissioni/bollettini/pdf/2012/10/11/leg.16.bol0718.data20121011.com02.pdf> accessed 1 September 2023.

and good practices from criminal liability in slight negligence cases (without excusing them from the obligation to pay damages, although compliance with guidelines was to be taken into account in quantifying the amount due).[67]

Unfortunately, this amendment raised several interpretation issues. First, scholars and some trial courts held the reference to art 2043 c c (ie to the general rule for tortious liability) implicitly quashed the *contatto sociale qualificato* doctrine, but the *Corte di cassazione* did not agree and continued to apply contract law rules to cases involving employed doctors.[68] Second, the use of statutory schedules for damages (which was not repealed by the Parliament) was difficult to reconcile with the new requirement to consider compliance with guidelines when quantifying compensation.[69]

Not surprisingly, the parliamentary debate on how to improve Italian medical malpractice law resumed in October 2013.[70] In 2015, the Ministry of Health established an advisory commission chaired by Professor Alpa, which suggested: applying tortious liability to cases involving employed doctors; limiting hospitals' right of recourse; fostering the use of liability insurance; and introducing a mandatory pre-trial order appointing an expert, court-appointed witness at an earlier stage of the dispute.[71] In the meantime, the parliamentary debate ended in 2017 with the adoption of the so-called *legge Gelli-Bianco.*[72] This act aimed at a comprehensive reform of medical malpractice law, addressing both criminal and civil liability, as well as some insurance, procedural and evidence issues, partly following the suggestions of the Alpa commission.

However, the results were rather poor from a criminal law perspective. Specifically, the legislature required healthcare professionals to follow the recommendations set forth in the guidelines published in the *Sistema nazionale per le linee guida* (national guidelines repository), and good clinical practices in the absence of those guidelines.[73] As concerns the application of

---

67 Art 3, co 1 *decreto Balduzzi* as modified by *legge 8 novembre 2012 n 189*: 'L'esercente la professione sanitaria che nello svolgimento della propria attività si attiene a linee guida e buone pratiche accreditate dalla comunità scientifica non risponde penalmente per colpa lieve. In tali casi resta comunque fermo l'obbligo di cui all'articolo 2043 del codice civile. Il giudice, anche nella determinazione del risarcimento del danno, tiene debitamente conto della condotta di cui al primo periodo'.

68 Carlo Masieri, 'La responsabilità civile dell'«esercente la professione sanitaria»' (2015) 4 Ricerche Giuridiche 103, 109–24.

69 'Il giudice, anche nella determinazione del risarcimento del danno, tiene debitamente conto della condotta di cui al primo periodo'.

70 Carlo Masieri, 'Novità in tema di responsabilita' sanitaria' (2017) Nuova Giur Civ Comm 752.

71 Ministero della Salute, *Commissione consultiva per le problematiche in materia di medicina difensiva e di responsabilita' professionale degli esercenti le professioni sanitarie* <www.quotidianosanita.it/allegati/allegato2684265.pdf> accessed 15 September 2023.

72 *Legge 8 marzo 2017, n 24.*

73 Art 5, co 1 *legge Gelli-Bianco*: 'Gli esercenti le professioni sanitarie, nell'esecuzione delle prestazioni sanitarie con finalità preventive, diagnostiche, terapeutiche, palliative, riabilitative

the aforementioned recommendations to the patient's specific condition, the healthcare professional who complies with them but nevertheless commits an '*imperizia*' ('unskilful conduct') shall be exempted from criminal liability.[74] As has been sharply pointed out, this is in fact an unsatisfactory wording.[75] Moreover, the *Cassazione* has further narrowed the scope of this statutory exemption, granting it only to those defendants whose *imperizia* was only slight and related to the performance, not the selection, of the medical treatment.[76]

As mentioned earlier, the *legge Gelli-Bianco* also dealt with civil liability.[77] The legislature confirmed the contractual analysis of the liability of hospitals but repealed the *contatto sociale qualificato* doctrine once applied by the judiciary in cases involving employed doctors – who can now only be sued in tort.[78] As explained in the first chapter, this entails the application of

---

e di medicina legale, si attengono, salve le specificità del caso concreto, alle raccomandazioni previste dalle linee guida pubblicate ai sensi del comma 3. (. . .) In mancanza delle suddette raccomandazioni', gli esercenti le professioni sanitarie si attengono alle buone pratiche clinico-assistenziali'.

74 Art 6 *legge Gelli-Bianco*, which introduced art 590-sexies c p: 'Qualora l'evento si sia verificato a causa di imperizia, la punibilità è esclusa quando sono rispettate le raccomandazioni previste dalle linee guida come definite e pubblicate ai sensi di legge ovvero, in mancanza di queste, le buone pratiche clinico-assistenziali, sempre che le raccomandazioni previste dalle predette linee guida risultino adeguate alle specificità del caso concreto'.

75 Cristiano Cupelli, 'Art 590-sexies c p', in Emilio Dolcini and Gian Luigi Gatta (eds), *Codice penale commentato* (5th edn, Wolters Kluwer 2021) 1268.

76 Cass pen sez un 21 dicembre 2017 n 8770, in Foro It 2018 II, 217.

77 Art 7 *legge Gelli-Bianco*: '1. La struttura sanitaria o sociosanitaria pubblica o privata che, nell'adempimento della propria obbligazione, si avvalga dell'opera di esercenti la professione sanitaria, anche se scelti dal paziente e ancorché non dipendenti della struttura stessa, risponde, ai sensi degli articoli 1218 e 1228 del codice civile, delle loro condotte dolose o colpose.

2. La disposizione di cui al comma 1 si applica anche alle prestazioni sanitarie svolte in regime di libera professione intramuraria ovvero nell'ambito di attività di sperimentazione e di ricerca clinica ovvero in regime di convenzione con il Servizio sanitario nazionale nonché attraverso la telemedicina.

3. L'esercente la professione sanitaria di cui ai commi 1 e 2 risponde del proprio operato ai sensi dell'articolo 2043 del codice civile, salvo che abbia agito nell'adempimento di obbligazione contrattuale assunta con il paziente. Il giudice, nella determinazione del risarcimento del danno, tiene conto della condotta dell'esercente la professione sanitaria ai sensi dell'articolo 5 della presente legge e dell'articolo 590-sexies del codice penale. (. . .)

4. Il danno conseguente all'attività della struttura sanitaria o sociosanitaria, pubblica o privata, e dell'esercente la professione sanitaria è risarcito sulla base delle tabelle di cui agli articoli 138 e 139 del codice delle assicurazioni private (. . .), integrate, ove necessario, con la procedura di cui al comma 1 del predetto articolo 138 e sulla base dei criteri di cui ai citati articoli, per tener conto delle fattispecie da esse non previste, afferenti alle attività di cui al presente articolo.

5. Le disposizioni del presente articolo costituiscono norme imperative ai sensi del codice civile'.

78 Guido Alpa, 'Ars interpretandi e responsabilità sanitaria a seguito della nuova legge Bianco-Gelli' (2017) Contr Impr 728, 730, 732–33; Enrico Moscati, 'Responsabilità sanitaria e teoria generale delle obbligazioni (note minime sui commi 1 e 3, prima frase, art. 7, l. 8 marzo 2017, n. 24)' (2018) Riv Dir Civ 829, 830, 833–34, 840–43, 847–50; Giulio Ponzanelli, 'Medical

different limitation periods (10 years for contractual liability; five years or the longer criminal law period, which is usually six years, for tortious liability) and different burdens of proof (for instance, in tort cases the claimant must prove negligence, whereas in contract cases the claimant must prove the existence of an obligation and merely allege that the defendant has breached it). As regards damages, the reform also extended the statutory schedules to the liability of hospitals and continued requiring compliance with guidelines be taken into account when quantifying compensation, at least when assessing the liability of employed doctors.[79]

In short, a practitioner who has either chosen the appropriate treatment in accordance with one of the guidelines entered in the national repository or acted in accordance with good clinical practices, but has nevertheless made a slight *imperizia* in carrying out that treatment, causing harm or even death to the patient, rather than being prosecuted, is liable for damages to the extent set out in the statutory schedules less an unspecified amount to be determined by the court.[80] Again, this is a rather complicated, if not poorly designed, mechanism.

Liability insurance became mandatory for all Italian physicians in 2011,[81] but some of the provisions of these policies were to be specified by a decree[82] that was not adopted until the end of 2023. Since 2014, the hospitals have been obliged to buy liability insurance (or at least to set up self-retention systems without requiring a specific governmental authorisation).[83] However, the carriers could still choose just not to underwrite the liability of doctors or hospitals (unlike what happens in other areas such as car insurance), suggesting the Italian mechanism was, again, poorly designed. By 2014, most Italian public

---

malpractice: la legge Bianco Gelli. Una premessa' (2017) Danno e Resp 268, 268–69, noting nonetheless that the tool for protecting the medical class, ie tortius liability instead of contractual liability, does not seem fit for the purpose; Enrico Quadri, 'Considerazioni in tema di responsabilità medica e di relativa assicurazione nella prospettiva dell'intervento legislativo' (2017) Resp Civ Prev 27, 37–38, casting doubts on the different treatment for independent practitioners, who answer in contract; Masieri (n 70) 752–53.

79 Most scholars believe compliance with guidelines irrelevant in the quantification of damages owed by the hospital: Carlo Granelli, 'La riforma della disciplina della responsabilità sanitaria: chi vince e chi perde?' (2017) Contratti 377, 379; Francesca Di Lella, 'Leges artis e responsabilità civile sanitaria' (2018) Nuova Giur Civ Comm II, 264, 270 fn 50; Nicola C Sacconi, 'Condotta dell'esercente la professione sanitaria e quantificazione del risarcimento' (2018) Resp Civ Prev 1351, 1360–63; according to Quadri (n 78) 37–38, independent practitioners fall outside of the scope of this provision, which thus results in unreasonable discrimination among physicians.

80 Masieri (n 61) 323–29.

81 Art 3, co 5, lett e *decreto legge 13 agosto 2011 n 138 conv con modif in legge 14 settembre 2011, n. 148*; art 5 *decreto del Presidente della Repubblica 7 agosto 2012, n. 137*.

82 Art 3, co 2 and 4 *decreto Balduzzi*.

83 Art 27, co 1-bis *decreto legge 24 giugno 2014 n. 90 conv con modif in legge 11 agosto 2014 n 114*; Velliscig (n 30) 238.

hospitals had already adopted risk retention systems.[84] However, risk retention systems set forth by Italian hospitals did not have adequate technical-economical features[85] nor asset segregation.[86] These healthcare facilities bought policies also containing considerable self-insured retention clauses, which may not work well in case of initial underestimation of the claims by the insured.[87]

The *legge Gelli-Bianco*[88] confirmed hospitals must have liability insurance or a self-retention system; the government was responsible for specifying the content of the policies, as well as the minimum requirements and the operational conditions of self-retention systems, whose assets are now deemed to be segregated by some scholars interpreting the reform.[89] The *legge Gelli-Bianco* also required hospitals to cover the civil liability of their employees towards patients. In turn, health professionals working for hospitals were only required to take out individual liability insurance covering their employers' right of recourse, allowed only when the employee acts with *dolo* (intentional harm) or *colpa grave* (gross negligence), and the amount recoverable is capped.[90] Direct action by the victim against the hospital's insurer was allowed,[91] at least theoretically. Claims made and extension clauses were made mandatory for medical and hospital liability policies.[92] A special fund, financed by a contribution from insurers, was established to compensate any damages exceeding the maximum coverage or where no policy exists,[93] and a subsequent amendment was supposed to help independent practitioners afford their own policies.[94]

All these new insurance law provisions, together with the shorter time limit and the defendant-oriented burden of proof of tortious liability, were aimed at relieving the class of employed doctors (who represent a very significant

---

84 Gianluca Romagnoli, 'Autoassicurazione della responsabilità medica: compatibilità con i principi di diritto interno ed europeo' (2015) Danno e Resp 329, 330.

85 Velliscig (n 30) 253–56.

86 Gianluca Romagnoli, 'Limiti di "praticabilità" della c.d. autoassicurazione della responsabilità medica da parte delle amministrazioni sanitarie', in Sara Landini (ed), *Autoassicurazione e gestione del rischio* (CESIFIN 2015) 67–70 <www.cesifin.it/wp-content/uploads/2016/12/AUTOASSICURAZIONE_E_GESTIONE_DEL_RISCHIO_22_09_15..pdf> accessed 6 October 2023.

87 Pierfrancesco Colaianni, 'Autoassicurazione e assicurazione nella responsabilità civile medica', in Landini (ed) (n 86) 43.

88 Art 10 *legge Gelli-Bianco*.

89 Velliscig (n 30) 281–89, 294–95.

90 Art 9 *legge Gelli-Bianco*.

91 Art 12 *legge Gelli-Bianco*.

92 Art 11 *legge Gelli-Bianco*.

93 Art 14 *legge Gelli-Bianco*.

94 Art 11, co 1, lett e *legge 11 gennaio 2018 n 3*, which inserted art 14, co 7-bis *legge Gelli-Bianco*.

proportion of all physicians in Italy)[95] from the pressure of litigation and the difficulties of the liability insurance market.

However, for some provisions of the *legge Gelli-Bianco* to enter into force, further detailed regulations had to be adopted by the government. For instance, direct action of the patient against the liability insurer depended on a decree specifying the content of insurance policies, as well as the requirements and operational conditions of hospitals' self-retention systems, which was not adopted until the end of 2023.[96]

From a procedural perspective, pre-trial mediation has been mandatory in medical malpractice cases since 2011.[97] Alternatively, the *legge Gelli-Bianco* allows the claimant to request a pre-trial order appointing a panel of at least two experts (one in legal medicine and one in the speciality at issue in the case)[98] with the task of ascertaining the claims arising from the non-performance of a contractual obligation or from a tort, as well as to facilitate the conciliation of the parties,[99] as mentioned in the first chapter. If no agreement is reached at this stage, the panel prepares a written report and the claimant can then start trial, during which both claimant and defendant can refer to the aforementioned report. If expertise is needed at the trial stage, the court shall always appoint a similar panel.[100]

The law also states that medical malpractice proceedings commenced after a pre-trial order must follow a sort of fast-track procedure,[101] while it seems that those starting after pre-trial mediation may still follow the general procedure.[102]

In 2022 and 2023, a reform of the Code of Civil Procedure entered into force[103] that, among other things, modified the pleadings stage and simplified how court-appointed experts are sworn in; it also enhanced the digitalisation of the filings.

The debate on medical malpractice law in Italy is far from over.

---

95 According to Ministero della Salute, *Annuario Statistico del Servizio Sanitario Nazionale. Assetto organizzativo, attività e fattori produttivi del SSN. Anno 2020* (2022) 83 <www.salute. gov.it/imgs/C_17_pubblicazioni_3245_allegato.pdf> accessed 14 September 2023, and to data published on the website of the *Istituto Nazionale di Statistica* (National Institute for Statistics) <http://dati.istat.it/Index.aspx?DataSetCode=DCIS_PERS_SANIT#> accessed 14 September 2023, in 2020 103,092 out of the 237,844 doctors registered in Italy were public hospitals' employees.

96 Art 12, co 6 and art 10, co 6 *legge Gelli-Bianco*; *decreto ministeriale 15 dicembre 2023 n 232, GU 1 marzo 2024 n 51*.

97 Art 5 *decreto legislativo 4 marzo 2010 n 28*.

98 Art 8, co 4 and art 15 *legge Gelli-Bianco*; art 696-bis c p c.

99 Art 8, co 3 *legge Gelli-Bianco*.

100 Art 15 *legge Gelli-Bianco*.

101 Art 8, co 3 *legge Gelli-Bianco*, and arts 281-decies and 281-undecies c p c.

102 Masieri (n 70) 769.

103 *Decreto legislativo 10 ottobre 2022 n 149; decreto legge 24 febbraio 2023 n 13 conv con modif in legge 21 aprile 2023 n 41.*

Since 2017, case law illustrates the existence of a new trend to allocate the burden of proving causation – which must be borne by the claimant also in contractual liability cases.[104]

During the Covid-19 pandemic, two criminal law provisions were adopted, shielding the healthcare professionals who administered the vaccines from prosecution and requiring *colpa grave* for negligent manslaughters and negligent bodily injuries committed during the public health emergency.[105] Yet, civil liability remained unchanged, despite legislative proposals.[106]

In 2022, although a draft bill was proposed to, among other things, reinstate contractual liability for all physicians, it was not put to a vote.[107]

Finally, in 2023 the Ministry of Justice established a new advisory commission to discuss the critical aspects of current Italian medical malpractice law and promote the debate on possible further reforms.[108]

Conclusions

From a comparative law perspective, the medical malpractice reforms in the Civil Law countries analysed in this chapter can first be distinguished according to their general purpose.

On the one hand, the German *Patientenrechtegesetz* was aimed primarily at codifying the solutions already found in case law in order to achieve greater transparency and legal certainty for the victims. On the other hand, the French and Italian statutes had a wider scope and pursued legal innovation, sometimes even repealing case law, as occurred in Italy with the *contatto sociale qualificato* doctrine.

---

104 Cass civ sez III 14 novembre 2017 n 26824, in Foro It 2018 I, 557ff; Cass civ sez III 26 luglio 2017 n 18392, in Foro It 2017 I, 3358ff.

105 Art 3 *decreto legge 1 aprile 2021 n 44*, and art 3-bis of the same *decreto legge*, introduced by art 1, co 1 *legge 28 maggio 2021 n 76*; Carlo M Masieri, 'Emergenza pandemica e (ir)responsabilità sanitaria' (2022) Resp Civ Prev 1304, 1310–11.

106 Giovanni Comandé, 'La responsabilità sanitaria al tempo del coronavirus ... e dopo' (2020) Danno e Resp 297, 303–05; Ugo Ruffolo, 'Le responsabilità mediche nell'emergenza sanitaria' (2021) Giur It 483, 484; Umberto Izzo, 'Responsabilità sanitaria e Covid-19: scenari di una possibile pandemia giudiziaria e risposte per prevenirla – I parte' (2020) Resp Civ Prev 1768, 1786–87.

107 *XVIII Legislatura – Atto Camera 1321 – Modifiche alla legge 8 marzo 2017, n. 24, al codice di procedura civile e alle disposizioni per la sua attuazione nonché alle norme di attuazione, di coordinamento e transitorie del codice di procedura penale, in materia di responsabilità sanitaria* <www.camera.it/leg18/126?tab=1&leg=18&idDocumento=1321&sede=&tipo=> accessed 15 September 2023.

108 Ministero della Giustizia, *Commissione d'Ippolito – Commissione per lo studio e l'approfondimento delle problematiche relative alla colpa professionale medica (28 marzo 2023) – Scheda di sintesi* <www.giustizia.it/giustizia/it/mg_1_36_0.page?contentId=COS42 4596> accessed 15 September 2023.

Legal scholars from all three countries have proposed adopting broad no-fault systems for medical malpractice, but today only France has such a system in place, and only for serious injuries. Strict liability remains sectoral. On the contrary, there is a general legislative trend towards confirming negligence as the main liability rule for medical malpractice, with the exception of the contractual analysis of the liability of hospitals and independent practitioners in Italy, which involves a lighter burden of proof for the claimant.

Regarding statutes of limitations, France and Germany sought uniformity, while Italy abandoned it by applying the tort analysis to the liability of employed doctors. There are good reasons for both solutions: a single limitation period promotes clarity and equality, while shortening the time limit for actions against employees may lead claimants to focus on the deep pockets of employers (ie hospitals), thus relieving doctors from the pressure of litigation. However, there is another important distinction to be made. The German *Schuldrechtsmodernisierungsgesetz* links the beginning of its 30-year limitation period to the act, breach of duty or other event that caused the injury. The 10-year limitation period under *loi Kouchner* starts from the consolidation of the injury, which can be a long and uncertain time after the wrongful act, and the same could be said of the 20-year long-stop that has theoretically applied to medical malpractice cases since 2016. The *legge Gelli-Bianco* does not appear to have even considered the fact that, in Italy, case law establishes limitation periods, be they five or 10 years, which do not begin to run until the aggrieved party learns the harm was caused by the intentional or negligent conduct of another, which can be much later than the medical treatment. Accordingly, only the German legislature has set a maximum period for bringing medical malpractice claims capable of meeting the actuarial needs of the insurance industry – which is essential for effective compensation of the victims.

Predictability of awards is another factor that facilitates the functioning of the insurance market. In this respect, scheduled damages are a very interesting solution, although the *decreto Balduzzi* and the *legge Gelli-Bianco* require to consider also compliance with clinical practice guidelines.

Although the risk of direct liability of employed doctors towards the patients is much lower in France than in Italy, both countries sought to relieve this class of clinicians of the costs of liability insurance, which was made compulsory for all healthcare providers.

This aspect of the reform was promisingly pursued by France, which, unlike Italy, created an underwriting obligation for insurance companies. Both countries allowed hospitals to adopt self-retention mechanisms, thus leaving open the possibility of doing without liability insurance. But French hospitals must obtain an authorisation from the government, which as of today has been granted just to the *Assistance Publique* in the Paris area, whereas Italian hospitals do not have this requirement; this is not to say they do not undergo regulatory guidance, which has been very recently adopted. Indeed, mixed systems might not work well if the scope of mandatory insurance and alternative risk retention differ, as such variance incentivises the use of insurance policies by high-risk healthcare providers only.[109]

Changes in civil procedure and in the law of evidence have been limited. The previous Civil Law features of court-appointed experts were confirmed. The German experience of the *Gutachterkommissionen* and of the *Schlichtungsstellen* probably inspired the French reform, while in Italy mandatory mediation or pre-trial court-appointed expert panels have been adopted. Therefore, in the face of long-lasting trials, the general trend is to entrust alternative dispute resolution bodies with the task of speeding up the resolution of medical malpractice disputes, albeit with the risk of creating a kind of parallel justice system.

As regards criminal law, both the French and the Italian legislatures felt the need to set more stringent conviction requirements. However, the *decreto Balduzzi* and the *legge Gelli-Bianco* adopted very complicated formulations, and the scope of the latter has been narrowed by the *Cassazione*, so this aspect of the Italian reform may end up having little impact.

Suggested Further Reading List

Coggiola N, 'Medical Liability Law in Italy' (2019) 23 Journal du Droit de la Santé et de l'Assurance – Maladie 45

Sebok A J, 'Recovery for Physical Harm: The Case of Medical Malpractice', in Bussani M, Sebok A J and Infantino M, *Common Law and Civil Law Perspectives on Tort Law* (OUP 2022)

Stauch M, 'The 2013 German Patients' Rights Act – Codifying Medical Malpractice Compensation' (2015) 6 JETL 85

Taylor S, *Medical Accident Liability and Redress in English and French Law* (CUP 2015)

109 Velliscig (n 30) 124–25.

3 The Aftermath of Reforms
What Has Changed?

France

Immediately following the enactment of the *loi Kouchner*,[1] some insurance companies left the market or charged higher premiums.[2] According to an enquiry conducted by a French public body, in 2001–02 there was a deterioration in the underwriting accounts, despite a high increase in insurance premiums for healthcare professionals, and there was also a contraction in the insurance offer due to the withdrawal of certain carriers from the market while claims experienced a steady growth, with compensation rising sharply in some categories of cases.[3]

Further contributions offer more detailed information.

Insurance premiums for surgeons rose by 60% in 2002, by 25% between 2002 and 2003 and by 39% between 2003 and 2004, followed by a movement of protest.[4]

By the beginning of 2003, specialists in foetal ultrasound, surgeons and Languedoc-Roussillon private hospitals filed complaints against liability insurance companies lamenting abuse of dominance, cartel and the deliberate creation of shortage in the coverage offer with consequent increase in premiums. However, the French trade commission dismissed these complaints in 2006.[5]

1 *Loi n°2002–303 du 4 mars 2002 relative aux droits des malades et à la qualité du système de santé.*

2 Irène Natowicz-Laurent, 'Les conséquences économiques de l'évolution du droit de la responsabilité civile médicale: un état des lieux' (2007) 117 Revue d'économie politique 963, 964.

3 Inspection générale des finances and Inspection générale des affaires sociales, *Conclusions du rapport d'enquête sur l'assurance de responsabilite civile medicale* (2004) <https://medias.vie-publique.fr/data_storage_s3/rapport/pdf/044000073.pdf> accessed 26 June 2023.

4 Régine Bercot and Alexandre Mathieu-Fritz, 'La crise de recrutement des chirurgiens français: entre mythes et réalités' (2007) 48 Revue française de sociologie 751, 759–61.

5 Conseil de la concurrence, *Décision n° 06-D-34 du 9 novembre 2006 relative à des saisines concernant le domaine de l'assurance de la responsabilité civile médicale* <www.autoritedela concurrence.fr/sites/default/files/commitments//06d34.pdf> accessed 21 September 2023.

DOI: 10.4324/9781003440277-4

In 2003, the French obstetricians working in private hospitals went on strike due to the high insurance premiums,[6] and the government provided financial aid for them and for other specialties so they could pay insurance premiums for that year.[7]

On 26 August 2004 the French government also promised to contribute to the stabilisation of premiums for surgeons and obstetrician/gynaecologists, but according to the unions this agreement has been left unfulfilled, leading to strikes in July 2006.[8] During the spring of the same year, a very relevant insurance carrier announced that in 2007 it would terminate all its contracts with gynaecologists and obstetricians and significantly increase their premiums.[9] Consequently, the government issued further financial aids for the coverage of surgeons and obstetricians/gynaecologists.[10]

Therefore, the French reforms of 2002 do not appear to have had a *per se* positive impact on the insurance market, at least initially and with regard to certain specialties.

According to some reports commissioned by French Ministries, in 2007 the situation had returned to normality,[11] and in 2011 the insurance market was working again.[12] But a report of 2021 to the French Senate, referring to data from the *Fédération française de l'assurance* (French Insurance Federation), noted that the loss ratio in the medical liability field has been rising steadily since 2013 and reached 103% in 2019, meaning the business is unprofitable.[13] As of today, there are 18 insurance companies in the medical malpractice sector, which is concentrated, with just five carriers accounting for 77% of the market in 2021.[14]

---

6 'French obstetricians strike' (2003) 326 BMJ 68.

7 Joël Moret-Bailly, 'Assurance, assurance-maladie et État: qui doit payer pour les fautes de médecins?' (2004) Resp civ et assur, alerte 11.

8 *Application du protocole d'accord du 24 août 2004 sur le chirurgie française. Résumé du rapport n° RM2006145P présenté par Christine d'Autume, membre de l'Inspection générale des affaires sociales* (2006) 1 < https://medias.vie-publique.fr/data_storage_s3/rapport/pdf/064000724.pdf> accessed 6 November 2023.

9 Pierre-Louis Bras, Christine d'Autume, Bernadette Roussille and Valerie Saintoyant, *L'assurance en responsabilité civile médicale* (2007) 3 <https://medias.vie-publique.fr/data_storage_s3/rapport/pdf/074000243.pdf> accessed 9 November 2023.

10 *Décret n° 2006–909 du 21 juillet 2006 relatif à l'accréditation de la qualité de la pratique professionnelle des médecins et des équipes médicales exerçant en établissements de santé, Décret n° 2006–1559 du 7 décembre 2006 modifiant les dispositions relatives à l'accréditation de la qualité de la pratique professionnelle des médecins et des équipes médicales exerçant en établissements de santé.*

11 Bras, d'Autume, Roussille and Saintoyant (n 9) 11.

12 Gilles Johanet, *L'assurance responsabilité civile des professionnels de santé* (2011) 3 <https://medias.vie-publique.fr/data_storage_s3/rapport/pdf/114000101.pdf> accessed 9 November 2023.

13 Catherine Procaccia, *Rapport d'information fait au nom de la commission des affaires sociales sur l'assurance responsabilité civile médicale des professionnels de santé libéraux* (2021) 12 <www.senat.fr/rap/r20-693/r20-6931.pdf> accessed 9 November 2023.

14 Anne-Marie Papeix, 'Contexte et ambitions de la loi About – Le point de vue de l'assureur' (2023) Resp civ et assur, dossier 17.

As already discussed in the first chapter, during the 1980s, the *Assistance Publique*, ie the public body entrusted with healthcare in the Paris area, received around 400 notifications by hospitals and requests from the victims together per year, budgeting in 1993 $2 million for malpractice damages.[15] A scholar found that in 2012 the same public body paid 17 million euros in compensation for medical accidents.[16] In 2014, it received 558 new filings and paid 13.2 million euros for damages to the victims of medical malpractice and reimbursement to their health insurance funds.[17] It seems that the same happened in 2015, but in 2016 the new filings were 676 and the *Assistance Publique* spent 15.4 million euros.[18] In 2015 and 2016, 50% of the procedures stemming out of those filings were out-of-court negotiations, another 30% were examined by the *commissions de conciliation et d'indemnisation* (conciliation and compensation commissions), while 15%, ie around 112 cases per year,[19] were brought to the administrative tribunals, which is less than in 1994, when the highest pre-reform score of 150 yearly lawsuits was recorded.[20] In 2023, the Director of Legal Affairs and Patients' Rights of the *Assistance Publique* reported numbers and typologies of claims similar to those of 2015–16.[21] So this very important public healthcare player receives today more filings than before the reforms, albeit they lead mostly to out-of-court procedures, and administrative tribunals seem to be less involved than in some past years. Nonetheless, the costs for the *Assistance Publique* have increased tremendously.

In 2009, the medical malpractice liability insurance premiums collected in France were 478 million euros.[22]

According to an article, in the same year *Le Sou Médical* and the *Mutuelle d'assurances du corps de santé français* (MACSF), that had established a coinsurance partnership named *Groupe des assurances mutuelles médicales* (GAMM) covering around 56% of all physicians working in France, received from their insured 1.66 notifications of possible bodily injuries per

---

15 Isabelle Durand-Zaleski, Jean-François Moreau, Elisabeth Conge and Claudine Blum-Boisgard, 'Medical Malpractice in France: The Effects of a Two-Fold Jurisdiction and the Case of Radiology' (1993) 28 Inves Radiol 459, 460.

16 Simon Taylor, *Medical Accident Liability and Redress in English and French Law* (CUP 2015) 78.

17 Assistance Publique – Hôpitaux de Paris, *Responsabilité médicale. Bilan de l'année 2014*, 2–3 <https://cme.aphp.fr/sites/default/files/CMEDoc/bilanresponsabilitemedicale2014.pdf> accessed 20 September 2023.

18 Assistance Publique – Hôpitaux de Paris, *Responsabilité médicale. Bilan de l'année 2016* (2017) 4 <https://cme.aphp.fr/sites/default/files/CMEDoc/cme7novembre2017_responsabilitemedicale_bilan.pdf> accessed 20 September 2023.

19 ibid 14.

20 Alain Levasseur, 'Les transactions: l'exemple de l'Assistance publique-Hôpitaux de Paris' (1997) AJDA 54.

21 Lydia Morlet-Haïdara, Marie-Charlotte Dalle, Isabelle Riaux, Pierre Jung et Patrick Flavin, 'Table ronde: focus sur la technique d'assurance' (2023) Resp civ et assur, dossier 24.

22 Johanet (n 12) 1.

100 doctors,[23] and this was actually less than the 2.33% scored in 1991.[24] But 2009 frequency is also less than the 1997–2007 period, so the decreasing trend predates the French reforms, because the frequency was already at ca 2% in 2000, and it then went at around 1.8%.[25]

This might be explained in part with the case law that at the beginning of the XXI century relieved doctors employed by private hospitals from most of the direct actions of the patients, and also with the obligation on the hospitals to cover the liability risk of their employees set up by the *loi Kouchner*, so that the insurance companies of the employers, not of their employees, are involved.[26]

According to the aforementioned article, the defendants insured by *Le Sou Médical* and *Groupe MACSF* lost around 50% of the civil trials in 2002, 2003 and 2004, getting to 68% in 2009, and in the same year one out of two doctors facing criminal charges has been found guilty.[27] Things seem to have gone differently in the past. We have already noted in the first chapter that between 1977 and 1991 79.05% of the civil trials and 86% of the criminal proceeding ended without a payment by the same insurers.[28] Although the elements taken into consideration are different (negative judicial outcomes after the reforms on the hand, and payment of claims before the reforms on the other hand), they can be compared, as they are arguably correlated (no insurer would have made payments had the defendants prevailed). Accordingly, there has been an increase in the rate of judicial defeats for doctors. This has been explained by the fact that after the *loi Kouchner* the cases of *aléa*, in which criminal and civil courts would have found for the defendants in the past, have been diverted to the no-fault scheme, nowadays allowing compensation, and so the incidence of good negligence cases tried by the judiciary has increased.[29]

As regards the interplay between different litigation systems, in 2009, 38.2% of the notifications received by *Le Sou Médical* and *MACSF* referred to extra-judicial requests for compensation, 23.7% to referrals to a conciliation and compensation commission, 32.6% to civil or administrative proceedings, and 5.5% to criminal proceedings.[30] Regarding the pre-reform period,

---

23 P Trouiller, E Lopard, J Mantz and T Farman, 'De la complication médicale à l'indemnisation du préjudice' (2012) 31 Ann Fr Anesth Réanim 626, 628.

24 Christine Le Clainche and Guy Poquet, *La responsabilité médicale et l'indemnisation du risque thérapeutique: Etat des lieux* (Centre de Recherche pour l'Étude et l'Observation des Conditions de Vie – CRÉDOC 1992) 13–14 <www.credoc.fr/download/pdf/Rapp/R128.pdf> accessed 4 July 2023.

25 A Najaf-Zadeha, F Dubosa, M Aurela, C Bons-Letouzeyc, R Amalbertic and A Martinot, 'Incidence des déclarations de plaintes envers les pédiatres' (2010) 17(2) Archives de pédiatrie 183.

26 ibid.

27 Trouiller, Lopard, Mantz and Farman (n 23) 628.

28 Le Clainche and Poquet (n 24) 18.

29 Trouiller, Lopard, Mantz and Farman (n 23) 628.

30 ibid.

we looked at a slightly different aspect, ie closed claims: between 1977 and 1991, 55% were out-of-court controversies, 31% civil trials and 14% criminal trials.[31] It thus seems that disputes are increasingly dealt with out-of-court.

A study focusing on claims filed against a hospital in Nancy between 2003 and 2007 highlighted that the *commissions de conciliation et d'indemnisation* were involved in more than one case out of three.[32]

Further research on the *commissions* highlighted that these played an increasingly important role between 2005 and 2009.[33] As of 2009, they dismissed 65.5% of the requests, while 63% of the decisions in favour of the claimants were *aléa thérapeutique* cases, whose compensation was another target of the reform.[34]

The *Commission nationale des accidents médicaux* (CNAMed), which is in charge, among other things, of ensuring that the rules are applied consistently by the regional commissions, published its own reports, which reveal that between 2006 and 2012 there has been an average increase of around 8% per year of cases filed with the commissions.[35]

In 2013, the increase was 1%.[36] As regards the outcomes for that year, 34% of the cases have been dismissed without getting to the merits;[37] of these, 62% were dismissed because the required threshold of seriousness of the injury. was clearly not met,[38] which means 21% of all cases. Only 44% of the opinions on the merits were in favour of the claimants, whereas 56% were not.[39] So, of all the opinions issued by the commissions in 2013, 34% were negative before the merits and 37% on the merits, which means an overall rate of negative decisions of 71%. 31% of the negative opinions on the merits were due to a lack of seriousness of the injury,[40] which means that another 11% of all cases did not reach that threshold, and so an overall lack of this requirement in 33% of all cases. It also seems that around 40% of the decisions in favour of the patients were *aléa thérapeutique* cases,[41] so this is considerably

31 Le Clainche and Poquet (n 24) 18.

32 Frédérique Claudot, François Allac, Jean-Pierre Villemot, Etienne Aliot, Henry Coudanea and Yves Juillière, 'Analysis of Patient Claims Related to Care in a University Cardiology Department over the Period 2003–2007' (2010) 103 Arch Cardiovasc Dis 595, 598.

33 Anne Laude, Jessica Pariente and Didier Tabuteau, *La judiciarisation de la santé* (Éditions de Santé 2012) 149–56.

34 Janine Barbot, Isabelle Parizot and Myriam Winancea, '"No-Fault" Compensation for Victims of Medical Injuries: Ten Years of Implementing the French Model' (2014) Health Policy 263, 241–43.

35 CNAMed, *Rapport annuel au parlement et au gouvernement année 2013* 17 <https://sante.gouv.fr/IMG/pdf/CNAMed2013.pdf> accessed 10 November 2023.

36 ibid 36.

37 ibid 19.

38 ibid 21.

39 ibid 25.

40 ibid 26.

41 ibid 29.

less than the 2009 result. But a subsequent report from the *Cour des comptes* (court of audit) said that in the 2011–15 period these kinds of cases were again at around 50%.[42]

The average duration of the proceedings in 2013 was 7.8 months,[43] ie slightly more than expected.

According to one commentor, in 2018 only 30% of the opinions from the commissions were favourable to the claimants.[44] Another article reports that in the same year the average duration of the commissions' proceedings was 8 months, and the number of parallel civil and administrative trials was rising.[45] Accordingly, as regards the commissions, the success rate of claims they managed and the duration of their proceedings was stable over the 2013–18 period.

From 2018, the number of claims filed with the commission has constantly decreased, and in 2022 this number dropped to 4,130, which is near the 2010 level.[46]

In 2022, the opinions for the patients were 35%, but the commissions took an average of 10 months per proceedings,[47] which means almost double the expected duration.

The *Observatoire des risques médicaux* (ORM) (observatory on medical risks) at the *Office national d'indemnisation des accidents médicaux, des affections iatrogènes et des infections nosocomiales* (ONIAM) (National Office for Compensation of Medical Accidents, Iatrogenic Diseases and Nosocomial Infections) collected reports from different sources regarding claims from 2009 up to 2014 valued at least € 15,000 and closed with a payment of at least 50% of their value: 74% of them came from insurance companies, which paid 63% of all sums received by the victims, whereas 24% of cases concerned the ONIAM.[48] Claims closed out-of-court were 88% of those reported by the ONIAM, whereas 51% of those closed by the insurers.[49] Half of the out-of-court settlements followed a procedure before a commission, but 22% of the

---

42 Cour des comptes, *L'indemnisation amiable des victimes d'accidents médicaux: une mise en œuvre dévoyée, une remise en ordre impérative* (2017) 80. <www.ccomptes.fr/sites/default/files/EzPublish/02-indemnisation-amiable-accidents-medicaux-Tome-1.pdf> accessed 10 November 2023.

43 ibid 35.

44 Caroline Lantero, 'Responsabilité hospitalière: les articulations entre procédure amiable et procédure contentieuse' (2019) AJDA 2391.

45 Thibaut Leleu, 'Vers la création d'un géant de l'indemnisation: à propos du rapport IGF/IGAS proposant la fusion de l'ONIAM et du FIVA' (2020) Resp civ et assur, étude 12.

46 ONIAM, *Rapport d'activité 2022* (2023) 14 <www.oniam.fr/medias/uploads/RA/ONIAM-RAPPORT_ACTIVITE_2022.pdf> accessed 13 November 2023.

47 ibid 4, 15–16.

48 ORM, *Rapport d'activité 2015. Années 2009 à 2014* (2015) 5–8, 11–14 <www.oniam.fr/medias/uploads/ORM/Rapport_ORM_2015__2009-2014.pdf> accessed 10 November 2023.

49 ibid 7.

opinions from the *commissions de conciliation et d'indemnisation* were followed by legal proceedings.[50]

According to the 2017 report from the *Cour des comptes*, the ONIAM refuses to abide by 8.5% of the opinions issued by the commissions in favour of the claimants,[51] and a subsequent report from the ONIAM reports a slight decrease of refusals in the following years.[52]

In the 2007–22 period, the courts confirmed 76% of the commissions' opinions brought to their attention, as well as 86% of ONIAM refusals.[53]

With regard to the administrative tribunals, a scholarly text, sponsored by a joint venture from the Ministry of Justice and the National Centre for Scientific Research, reported that there have been constantly around 4 cases per 100,000 admissions in public hospitals between 2000 and 2006.[54] However, one might also look to the evolution of their respective trends. So from the same data it can be calculated, for instance, that yearly requests for pre-trial orders filed with the administrative tribunals went from 127 in 2000 to 189 in 2006, ie grew by 49%, whereas yearly admissions in public hospitals were 14,182,205 in 2000 and 15,023,075 in 2006, or a mere 6% increase.[55] New trials scored +25%, from 256 in 2000 to 320 in 2006.[56] A previous study on the 1999–2004 period reported there were many more pending cases.[57]

Looking to information about the private sector,[58] it can be observed that between 2000 and 2006 new trials in the *tribunaux de grande instance* were stationary, while hospital admissions and medical acts were slightly rising.

As regards the outcome, 16.3% of civil court decisions issued from 1999 to 2009 were in favour of the defendants, while 42.9% were for the claimants.[59] These results are lower than those of 1992,[60] meaning that nowadays fewer civil cases end with a judgment and thus perhaps settlements are more frequent. Moreover, from 1999 to 2009, judgments are increasingly in favour of the patients, both in administrative tribunals and in civil courts.[61] This finding is in line with information from doctors' insurers.

---

50 ibid 8.
51 Cour des comptes (n 42) 80.
52 ONIAM (n 46) 18.
53 ibid 22.
54 Laude, Pariente and Tabuteau (n 33) 27–28.
55 ibid 23, 27.
56 ibid 134.
57 Laurence Helmlinger and Dominique Martin, 'La judiciarisation de la médecine, mythe et réalité' (2004) 5 Les Tribunes de la santé 39, 44.
58 Laude, Pariente and Tabuteau (n 33) 55, 134.
59 ibid 52–53.
60 Dominique Thouvenin, *La responsabilité médicale: Analyse des données statistiques disponibles et des arrêts rendus par la Cour de cassation et le Conseil d'Etat de 1984 à 1992* (Flammarion Médecine-Sciences 1995) 22.
61 Laude, Pariente and Tabuteau (n 33) 136.

The authors of the aforementioned book, which can be considered an excellent example for further quantitative research on medical malpractice, looked to several sources (courts and tribunals, conciliation commissions, insurance companies, public bodies, etc) and found an overall decrease in litigation from 2004 to 2006.[62]

As of 2015, the average duration of medical malpractice trials in both administrative tribunals and civil courts was less than two years.[63] We saw that the pre-reforms duration of medical malpractice trials in civil courts was more or less the same.[64]

All claims considered in the Nancy study were brought well before the limitation period deadline,[65] while according to other sources around 75% of claims at national level are filed within two years of the accident.[66] So the legislative amendment of the statute of limitations in France could perhaps be deemed of little relevance.

Some aspects of the French reforms have been criticised. Commentors assert that legal concepts, including that of *aléa thérapeutique*, are still not defined by the statutes, so that there is uncertainty in courts' decisions and variability in the outcome of cases examined by the commissions.[67] There are also complaints about the threshold of compensable harm, which is deemed too high.[68] It has been pointed out that the *commissions de conciliation et d'indemnisation* adopt several different interpretations of the rules,[69] because the CNAMed did not have the means to perform its tasks.[70] The commissions have also been questioned for lack of impartiality, eg for the director of ONIAM being also a member of the commission.[71] Moreover, it has been

---

62 ibid 147ff, 199.

63 Cour des comptes (n 42) 84.

64 Thouvenin (n 60) 23–24.

65 Claudot, Allac, Villemot, Aliot, Coudanea and Juillière (n 32) 599.

66 ORM (n 48) 7, 17.

67 Barbot, Parizot and Winancea (n 34) 243–44; Jonas Knetsch, 'The French Medical Accident Compensation Scheme: A Critical Assessment of the Patients' Rights Act of 4 March 2002', in Dobrochna Bach-Golecka (ed), *Compensation Schemes for Damages Caused by Healthcare and Alternatives to Court Proceedings: Comparative Law Perspectives* (Springer 2021) 187; Bertrand Debono, Carole Gerson, Thierry Houselstein, Lynda Lettat-Ouatah, Renaud Bougeard, and Nicolas Lonjon, 'Litigations Following Spinal Neurosurgery in France: "Out-of-Court System," Therapeutic Hazard, and Welfare State' (2020) 49(5) Neurosurg Focus E11, 7–8 <https://doi.org/10.3171/2020.8.FOCUS20582> accessed 20 September 2023.

68 Alain-Michel Ceretti and Laure Albertini, *Bilan et propositions de réformes de la loi du 4 mars 2002 relative aux droits des malades et à la qualité du système de santé* (2011) 219–25 <www.vie-publique.fr/rapport/31615-bilan-et-propositions-de-reformes-de-la-loi-du-4-mars-2002-relative-aux> accessed 9 November 2023; Simon Taylor, 'Providing Redress for Medical Accidents in France: Conflicting Aims, Effective Solutions?' (2011) 2 JETL 57, 65–68.

69 Taylor (n 16) 71–72.

70 Cour des comptes (n 42) 75, 78–79.

71 Ceretti and Albertini (n 68) 231–33; Stéphanie Porchy-Simon, 'Vingt ans de coexistence de la responsabilité et de la solidarité: bilan prospectif' (2022) Resp civ et assur, dossier 10.

observed that the ONIAM and the courts can award different amounts of damages for the same kind of injuries.[72]

On this topic, it is worth noticing that the French reforms did not address the problem of compensation, except for wrongful life cases. The ONIAM collected data on damages for bodily injuries awarded by the courts, and published a *référentiel* (reference system), a non-binding tool, which is useful for quantifying damages.[73] However, the civil courts widely adopted a different set of criteria, ie the *Dintilhac* nomenclature concerning the different heads of loss that can be compensated in the event of bodily injury,[74] which gained a *de facto* binding force.[75] Until 2013, administrative tribunals had their own quantification criteria, but afterwards they began using the *Dintilhac* nomenclature.[76] However, a recent study showed that there is still a lack of uniformity when courts apply the tools for quantifying damages.[77]

In 2004, a study on preventable adverse events has been conducted at the national level.[78] Data from 8,754 admissions/patients, making a total of 35,234 hospital days, was collected and analysed: 416 patients (4.75%) suffered a total of 450 serious adverse events (5.14%), 195 of which occurred prior to hospitalisation, with 86 (46.2%) considered avoidable, whereas the other 255 adverse events occurred during hospitalisation, of which 95 (35.4%) were deemed avoidable.[79] Accordingly, both the incidence of adverse events and preventable adverse events seem to be lower than that found in previous French studies.

The authors of the 2004 study also estimated that during the same year in France between 315,000 and 440,000 hospital admissions were caused by adverse events, of which between 125,000 and 205,000 were avoidable, whereas 350,000 to 450,000 adverse events occurred during hospital stays, of which between 120,000 and 190,000 were preventable.[80] So it is worth noting that the 2004 estimated preventable adverse events were far more than the medical

---

72 Christophe Radé, 'La loi Kouchner a 10 ans (déjà)' (2012) Resp civ et assur, alerte 5; Knetsch (n 67) 189–90.

73 Terry Olson and Thomas Argent, 'Responsabilité, assurance et solidarité en matière sanitaire' (2005) AJDA 2226.

74 Jean-Pierre Dintilhac, *Rapport du groupe de travail chargé d'élaborer une nomenclature des préjudices corporels* (2005) <https://sante.gouv.fr/IMG/pdf/Rapport_groupe_de_travail_nomenclature_des_prejudices_corporels_de_Jean-Pierre_Dintilhac.pdf> accessed 14 November 2023.

75 Matthieu Robineau, 'Le statut normatif de la nomenclature Dintilhac des préjudices' (2010) JCP G, doctr. 612; Hugues Adida-Canac, 'Le contrôle de la nomenclature Dintilhac par la Cour de cassation' (2011) D 1497; Jonas Knetsch, 'La désintégration du préjudice moral' (2015) D 443.

76 Philippe Brun and Olivier Gout, 'Responsabilité civile' (2015) D 124; Caroline Lantero, 'Les consolidations du droit de la responsabilité hospitalière' (2020) AJDA 714.

77 Christophe Quézel-Ambrunaz, 'La réparation des préjudices laissés par les cicatrices. Étude statistique' (2020) D 2248.

78 Philippe Michel et alii, *Étude nationale sur les évènements indésirables graves liés aux soins* (2006) 15, 25 <https://drees.solidarites-sante.gouv.fr/sites/default/files/2020-10/dtee60.pdf> accessed 13 November 2023.

79 ibid 28–30.

80 ibid 53, 59.

malpractice cases actually filed with the conciliation and compensation commissions (n=3453)[81] as well as those brought to courts during the same year either seeking pre-trial orders or starting a trial (n=5,570).[82]

After the reforms, some research on defensive medicine has been performed, showing that around 11% of the French neurosurgeons refused to perform risky operations due to the fear of complaints.[83] However, it must be recalled that according to French sociologists the subjective perceived risk of litigation, which is at the core of most of the studies on defensive medicine, may not be related to the actual dimensions of litigation.[84]

Germany

It seems that the German medical malpractice reform did not have an immediate positive effect on insurance premiums, especially with regard to midwives.[85]

The *Gesamtverband der Deutschen Versicherungswirtschaft* (GDV) (the German insurance association) reports that nowadays there are around 30 companies in the medical malpractice liability market, 12 of which participated in a survey on around 250 major medical malpractice claims from the 2003–20 period, during which the average claims expenditure for these claims doubled from 1.3 million euros to 2.6 million euros.[86] A member of the board of directors of *Deutsche Ärzteversicherung*, a company specialised in medical liability insurance, stated 10 years after the enactment of the *Patientenrechtegesetz* (patients' rights act) that the reform did not have an impact on claims expenditures.[87] Nonetheless, the following information indicates that the number of medical malpractice claims is decreasing.

The *Schlichtungsstellen* (conciliation commissions) and the *Gutachterkommissionen* (expert commissions), which were not affected by the German medical malpractice reform, still contribute to the out-of-court solutions of disputes, as around 90% of their opinions are accepted by the parties; negligence is found in 30% of cases and causation in 25%.[88] However, something

81 ONIAM (n 46) 14.

82 Laude, Pariente and Tabuteau (n 33) 148.

83 B Debono, O Hamel, A Guillain, A Durand, M Rué, P Sabatier, G Lonjon and G Drang, on behalf of French Society of Private Neurosurgeons (SFNCL), 'Impact of Malpractice Liability among Spine Surgeons: A National Survey of French private Neurosurgeons' (2020) 66 Neurochirurgie 219, 222.

84 Janine Barbot and Emmanuelle Fillion, 'La «médecine défensive»: critique d'un concept à succès' (2006) 24(2) Sciences sociales et santé 5, 10–11.

85 P Soergel, O Schöffski, P Hillemanns, U Hille-Betz and S Kundu, 'Increasing Liability Premiums in Obstetrics – Analysis, Effects and Options' (2015) 75 Geburtsh Frauenheilk 367, 369–70.

86 Marco Lonsing and Nils Hellberg, 'Superimposed Inflation hält an' (2022) VW 66.

87 Jörg Kieker, 'Patientenrechtegesetz 2.0 aus der Sicht eines Schadenversicherers' (2023) 41 MedR 101.

88 Marina Tamm, 'Außergerichtliche Streitbeilegung bei der Arzthaftung: Hat die Mediation neben der Schlichtung eine Chance?' (2017) GesR 764, 765.

seems to have changed: a recent article referring to the statistics from the German Medical Association said that 10,839 applications were submitted to the commissions in 2018 and 10,705 in 2019,[89] which would mean a decreasing trend in their activities. This is more evident if one looks at the entire post-reform period, ie from 2013 to 2021, the latest available year: cases filed yearly went from 12,173 down to 8,449,[90] or −30%.

The number of advisory assignments entrusted to the *Medizinische Dienst der Krankenversicherung* (MDK) went from 12,483 in 2012 to 14,000 in 2018, the year in which malpractice was found in 24.7% of cases,[91] although it must be noticed that causation was certain only in 19.8% of cases.[92] The following year, the assignments increased to 14,553, negligence was found in 25.3% of cases, along with causation in just 20.3% of cases.[93] Numbers were more or less the same in 2020, although the assignments decreased to 14,000.[94] The same was true for 2021 and 2022, with around 13,000 assignments per year.[95]

The number of medical malpractice cases decided by the German civil courts continued to increase after the reform, peaking at 11,046 in 2015[96]

---

89 Peter Glanzmann, 'Schlichtungsstellen und Gutachterkommissionen für Fragen ärztlicher Haftpflicht' (2021) 50 Orthopäde 159, 160.

90 See the Bundesärztekammer's website <www.aerztekammern-schlichten.de/statistik> accessed 16 November 2023.

91 J Heberer and M Eicher, 'Schadenmanagement aus Sicht des Juristen. Top 7 der Fehler im Arzthaftungsrecht' (2020) 123 Der Unfallchirurg 6.

92 Medizinischer Dienst des Spitzenverbandes Bund der Krankenkassen e.V. (MDS) and MDK Bayern, *Jahresstatistik 2018. Behandlungsfehler-Begutachtung der MDK-Gemeinschaft* (2019) 8 <https://md-bund.de/fileadmin/dokumente/Pressemitteilungen/2019/2019_05_16/2019-08-12_Behandlungsfehlerbegutachtung_Jahresstatistik_2018_PDF_UA.pdf> accessed 15 November 2023.

93 Medizinischer Dienst des Spitzenverbandes Bund der Krankenkassen e.V. (MDS) and MDK Bayern, *Jahresstatistik 2019. Behandlungsfehler-Begutachtung der MDK-Gemeinschaft* (2020) 6–7, 8 <https://md-bund.de/fileadmin/dokumente/Pressemitteilungen/2020/2020_06_25/20_06_25_MDK-Behandlungsfehlerbegutachtung_Jahresstatistik_2019_barrierefrei.pdf> accessed 15 November 2023.

94 Medizinischer Dienst des Spitzenverbandes Bund der Krankenkassen e.V. (MDS) and Medizinischer Dienst Bayern, *Behandlungsfehler-Begutachtung der Gemeinschaft der Medizinischen Dienste. Jahresstatistik 2020* (2021) 9 <https://md-bund.de/fileadmin/dokumente/Pressemitteilungen/2021/2021_10_12/4_FIN_-_MD_BEHANDLUNGSFEHLER_BF.pdf> accessed 15 November 2023.

95 Medizinischer Dienst Bund and Medizinischer Dienst Bayern, *Behandlungsfehler-Begutachtung der Gemeinschaft der Medizinischen Dienste Jahresstatistik 2021* (2022) 9 <https://md-bund.de/fileadmin/dokumente/Pressemitteilungen/2022/2022_06_30/22_06_30_PK_BHF_Jahresstatstik_BEHANDLUNGSFEHLER_2021_BF.pdf> accessed 15 November 2022; Medizinischer Dienst Bund and Medizinischer Dienst Bayern, *Behandlungsfehler-Begutachtung der Gemeinschaft der Medizinischen Dienste. Jahresstatistik 2022* (2023) 9 <https://md-bund.de/fileadmin/dokumente/Pressemitteilungen/2023/2023_08_17/PK_BHF_2022_Jahresstatistik.pdf> accessed 15 November 2022.

96 Statistisches Bundesamt, *Rechtspflege Zivilgerichte 2015* (2016) 18, 48 <www.statistische bibliothek.de/mir/servlets/MCRFileNodeServlet/DEHeft_derivate_00027207/2100210157004.pdf> accessed 15 November 2023.

before slightly decreasing to 9,992 in 2022, which is less than the 2012 result but still more than almost all the years in the 2004–12 period. And the average yearly number of cases from 2013 to 2022 is around 10,450, which is more than the 9,700 case yearly average registered between 2004 and 2012.

It must be stressed that the 2013 reform did not modify institutional aspects. Consequently, it was not able to channel the new disputes towards out-of-court solutions, some of which show clear signs of distress. If one confronts the 2013–21 series from the different sources, s/he will see that filings with the conciliation and expert commissions are constantly decreasing, while the MDK assignments peaked in 2016 and then had a less straight decrease, and the amount of courts' decisions has been more stable.

Another aspect must be observed: with time there are fewer and fewer cases at the *Amtsgericht*, the court for lower value cases, having been just 1,131 in 2021,[97] which according to a scholar means that medical malpractice victims are seeking ever greater awards.[98]

German judges have been left in charge of quantifying damages for pain and suffering, and they do not refer to uniform scheduled damages. They award these sums considering the seriousness of the injury, but not the age of the victim.[99]

The 2013 statute raised some interpretative problems, eg about the definition of the standard of care or the effects of the duty to disclose possible medical errors.[100] And from 2017 onwards, there has been some debate on possible further medical malpractice reforms.[101]

Italy

Before analysing the current scenario in Italy, some caveats might be useful.

The *legge Gelli-Bianco* of 2017,[102] ie the last Italian medical malpractice reform, is very recent. As we will see, this means that a share of accidents, which possibly occurred after its enactment, have not yet generated a claim.

97 Statistisches Bundesamt, *Rechtspflege Zivilgerichte 2021* (2022) 18 <www.statistischebibliothek. de/mir/servlets/MCRFileNodeServlet/DEHeft_derivate_00070926/2100210217004.pdf> accessed 15 November 2023.

98 Dominique Püster, *Entwicklungen der Arzthaftpflichtversicherung* (Springer 2013) 76.

99 Magdalena Flatscher-Thöni, Andrea M Leiter and Hannes Winner, 'Are Pain and Suffering Awards (Un-)predictable? Evidence from Germany' (2015) Working Papers in Economics and Finance University of Salzburg, No. 2015–02 <http://hdl.handle.net/10419/122168> accessed 15 November 2023.

100 Andreas Spickhoff, 'Die Arzthaftung im neuen bürgerlich-rechtlichen Normenumfeld: Eine erste Zwischenbilanz' (2015) 33 MedR 845, 848–49; Christian Katzenmeier, 'Patientenrechtegesetz 2.0? – Haftungsrecht' (2023) 41 MedR 118, 120.

101 Katzenmeier (n 100) 119, 124.

102 *Legge 8 marzo 2017, n 24.*

From a legal perspective, the scope and effectiveness of the very same act deserve some attention. In 2019, the *Cassazione* held that the tort law analysis of the employed doctors' liability does not apply to facts committed before the *legge Gelli-Bianco* entered into force:[103] a share of claims brought after the reform still refer to those previous facts, and is thus framed in the purview of contract law, with a burden of proof and a time limit favourable to the claimants. It must also be recalled that other parts of the *legge Gelli-Bianco*, eg the direct action of the patient against the liability insurer,[104] to become effective, required more detailed regulations (which were not adopted until the end of 2023). Scheduled damages followed a different path: they were adopted in the medical malpractice field for the first time with the *decreto Balduzzi* of 2012;[105] then they were extended to hospitals' liability with the 2017 law;[106] in 2019, the *Cassazione* surprisingly held that they are applicable even to injuries occurred before both Acts, ie to all pending cases, provided *res judicata* on damages has not been reached.[107]

Finally, in 2020 and 2021, access to healthcare was influenced by the Covid-19 pandemic; since Covid-19 may have also hindered medical malpractice litigation, this should be borne in mind when considering data from that period.

Still, multiple sources offer interesting information on the current status of medical malpractice in Italy.

As regards insurance, according to a 2022 report from the *Istituto per la Vigilanza sulle Assicurazioni* (IVASS) (the Italian supervisory authority for insurance), in 2021, five companies collected 79% of premiums nationwide, and 99% of those were paid by public hospitals.[108] Compared to 2017, the average cost of premiums increased by 35% for public hospitals, while decreasing for private hospitals (−56%) and for doctors (−30%).[109] Accordingly, after the *legge Gelli-Bianco*, although the Italian liability insurance market is even more concentrated, policies have become more affordable for private hospitals and, at least apparently, also for practitioners. However, it should be recalled that the 2017 reform made liability insurance

---

103 Cass civ sez III 11 novembre 2019 n 28994, in Foro It – Spec Iss 2020, 1, 377; on the criminal law aspects, see Fabio Basile and Pier Francesco Poli, 'La responsabilità per "colpa medica" a cinque anni dalla legge Gelli-Bianco – Responsibility For "Medical Malpractice" Five Years after the Gelli-Bianco Law' (2022) (1) Dir Pen Cont Riv Trim 79, 97–100.
104 Art 12, co 6 and art 10, co 6 *legge Gelli-Bianco*.
105 Art 3, co 3 *decreto legge 13 settembre 2012, n 158 conv con modif in legge 8 novembre 2012, n 189*.
106 Art 7, co 4 *legge Gelli-Bianco*.
107 Cass civ sez III 11 novembre 2019 n 28990, in Foro It – Spec Iss 2020, 1, 377.
108 IVASS, *I rischi da responsabilità civile generale e sanitaria in Italia* (2022) XIV Bollettino statistico 15–16 <www.ivass.it/pubblicazioni-e-statistiche/statistiche/bollettino-statistico/2022/n_14_2022/Bollettino_rcg_rcsanitaria.pdf> accessed 20 November 2023.
109 ibid 5.

mandatory for employed doctors only for *colpa grave*, ie gross negligence, and it refers only to the recourse of their employers;[110] as a result, the new compulsory policies are likely cheaper than the old ones, which provided full cover for all negligence claims.

Since 2012, and with the sole exception of 2017, malpractice claims filed with insurance companies decreased from 33,785 to 17,208 per year as of 2021.[111] However, this data must be matched with the extent of litigation managed directly by public hospitals, which in the same years have massively opted for full risk retention systems or policies with considerable self-insured retention clauses.

On this point, IVASS observed that self-retention by public hospitals peaked in 2017, and in the last four years some 13 public hospitals returned to insurance; nonetheless, in 2020 the self-retention funds were twice the amount of insurance premiums paid by hospitals.[112]

The *legge Gelli-Bianco* stressed the importance of data collection on adverse events and malpractice claims with regard to healthcare facilities both at the regional and national level,[113] and as of today this has worked well with public hospitals.

As regards 2017, 20 out of 21 Italian regions shared data concerning their public facilities: these received 11,390 claims,[114] while just 6,572 were registered by their insurers,[115] meaning that almost half of the litigation against public hospitals was not covered by a policy. 84.9% of claims came as an out-of-court request for compensation to the facilities, 2.4% referred to mediation, 8.0% were civil trials and 4.7% criminal proceedings,[116] with an average lag of 2.5 years between the event and the claim.[117]

In 2018, public hospitals stated to have received 11,951 claims:[118] this is more than the previous year, but it might be due to a stronger participation of

---

110 Art 10, co 4 *legge Gelli-Bianco*.

111 IVASS, *I rischi da responsabilità civile generale e sanitaria in Italia* (n 108) 18–19; IVASS, *Tavole statistiche – r.c. sanitaria* (2022) tab 4 <www.ivass.it/pubblicazioni-e-statistiche/statistiche/bollettino-statistico/2022/n_14_2022/Allegato_B_RC_SANITARIA.xlsb> accessed 20 November 2023.

112 IVASS (n 108) 17 fn 25, 20–22.

113 Art 2, co. 4 and art 3 *legge Gelli-Bianco*.

114 Osservatorio nazionale delle buone pratiche sulla sicurezza nella sanità, *Relazione annuale dicembre 2018* (2018) 37 <www.senato.it/service/PDF/PDFServer/DF/343448.pdf> accessed 21 November 2023.

115 IVASS, *Tavole statistiche* (n 111) tab 4.

116 Osservatorio nazionale delle buone pratiche sulla sicurezza nella sanità, *Indicatori per la sicurezza delle cure. Dicembre 2018* (2018) 59 <www.senato.it/service/PDF/PDFServer/DF/343448.pdf> accessed 21 November 2023.

117 ibid 62.

118 Osservatorio nazionale delle buone pratiche sulla sicurezza nella sanità, *Relazione 2019* (2019) 40 <www.buonepratichesicurezzasanita.it/images/RELAZIONE2019/Relazione_sintetica.pdf> accessed 21 November 2023.

the regions in this data collection. The same year, insurers were involved in just 6,357 of claims concerning hospitals,[119] ie less than in 2017. No data about 2019 appears available.

In 2020, Italian public hospitals registered 9,675 claims,[120] with a slight increase in the incidence of civil trials and a very slight decrease in criminal proceedings compared to 2017,[121] while the length of the period between the event and the claim was stable.[122] There were 5,716 claims registered by insurance companies and concerning the liability of public hospitals in the same year.[123]

The last available data refers to 2021, when new claims received by those facilities were 10,639,[124] back on the rise, while carriers registered 5,376 claims related to public hospitals' liability, which were thus fewer than the previous year.[125] The procedural paths matched those registered in 2020, but the average lag between the event and the claim slightly decreased.[126]

Yet, it must be recalled that the same claim can start as an out-of-court request for compensation and become a civil trial, that a pre-trial order or a mediation is required before a civil trial, and that parallel criminal and civil trials are allowed in Italy, but none of these aspects seem to have been considered in this dataset.

The frequency of claims against Italian public hospitals increased from 18.5 each 10,000 admissions in 2017[127] to 19.6 in 2020,[128] which is lower than the 21.5 frequency scored in 2015.

Taking into consideration all accidents to patients, workers and all third parties, in 2017 the average paid sum was € 61,412 for personal injuries and € 254,205 for death cases;[129] in 2018, it was € 58,497 and € 257,748 respectively;[130] no data concerning the following years seems available.

---

119 IVASS, *Tavole statistiche* (n 111) tab 4.
120 Osservatorio nazionale delle buone pratiche sulla sicurezza nella sanità, *Relazione annuale. Dicembre 2021* (2021) 56 <https://documenti.camera.it/_dati/leg18/lavori/documentiparlamentari/IndiceETesti/242/002/INTERO.pdf> accessed 21 November 2023.
121 ibid 92.
122 ibid 99.
123 IVASS, *Tavole statistiche* (n 111) tab 4.
124 Osservatorio nazionale delle buone pratiche sulla sicurezza nella sanità, *Relazione annuale. Dicembre 2022* (2022) 19 <www.senato.it/service/PDF/PDFServer/DF/427999.pdf> accessed 21 November 2023.
125 IVASS, *Tavole statistiche* (n 111) tab 4.
126 Osservatorio nazionale delle buone pratiche sulla sicurezza nella sanità, *Relazione annuale. Dicembre 2022* (n 124) 18, 22.
127 Osservatorio nazionale delle buone pratiche sulla sicurezza nella sanità, *Relazione 2019* (n 118) 35.
128 Osservatorio nazionale delle buone pratiche sulla sicurezza nella sanità, *Relazione annuale. Dicembre 2021* (n 120) 62.
129 Osservatorio nazionale delle buone pratiche sulla sicurezza nella sanità, *Indicatori per la sicurezza delle cure. Dicembre 2018* (n 116) 56.
130 Osservatorio nazionale delle buone pratiche sulla sicurezza nella sanità, *Relazione 2019* (n 118) 36.

The last risk mapping of the Lombardia healthcare system, published by the Directorate General of that region together with an insurance broker, shows that medical malpractice claims decreased every year from 1,684 in 2012 to 996 in 2020.[131] Their frequency decreased from 13.59 claims each 10,000 hospital admissions in 2012 to 10.56 in 2019.[132] However, except for 2016, the average payment for damages by the hospitals in Lombardia grew constantly,[133] and quite significantly: one can calculate a yearly average increase of around 4%. 85% of the claims are brought by the fifth year after the event.[134]

In Emilia-Romagna, claims filed in 2018 were more than those in 2017, but in 2019 the number decreased again to 2017 levels,[135] compared to which 2020, 2021 and 2022 showed a lower number of claims.[136] Claims' frequency in the last three years seems quite constant in that region.[137]

The claims concerning the hospitals of the *Azienda Provinciale per i Servizi Sanitari della Provincia Autonoma di Trento* (Provincial Agency for Health Services of the Autonomous Province of Trento) filed between 2013 and the first semester of 2022 also have been analysed;[138] 70% of claims are made by the third year following the event.[139] The yearly number of claims

---

131 Regione Lombardia and Aon S.p.A. Insurance & Reinsurance Brokers, *Mappatura del rischio del Sistema Sanitario Regionale. Risultati diciassettesima edizione 31/12/2020* (2021) 61 <www.regione.lombardia.it/wps/wcm/connect/7bcf1866-49ab-42cf-93de-2f19d67ecf03/XVII+ Edizione+Mappatura+regionale.pdf?MOD=AJPERES&CACHEID=ROOTWORKSPACE-7bcf1866-42cf-93de-2f19d67ecf03-nQ8.yRB> accessed 21 November 2023.

132 ibid.

133 ibid 116.

134 ibid 62.

135 Regione Emilia-Romagna – Centro per la Gestione del Rischio Sanitario e la Sicurezza del paziente – Osservatorio Regionale per la Sicurezza delle Cure, *Secondo report regionale sulle fonti informative per la sicurezza delle cure. Anno 2019* 13 <https://salute.regione.emilia-romagna.it/assistenza-ospedaliera/sicurezza-cure/il-sistema-per-la-sicurezza-delle-cure-nella-regione-emilia-romagna/report-2019.pdf> accessed 22 November 2023.

136 Regione Emilia-Romagna – Centro per la Gestione del Rischio Sanitario e la Sicurezza del paziente – Osservatorio Regionale per la Sicurezza delle Cure, *Quinto report regionale sulle fonti informative per la sicurezza delle cure. Anno 2022* 18 <https://salute.regione.emilia-romagna.it/assistenza-ospedaliera/sicurezza-cure/le-fonti-informative-per-la-sicurezza-delle-cure/quinto-report-fonti-informative-sicurezza-cure_anno-2022.pdf/@@download/file/Quinto%20report%20fonti%20informative%20sicurezza%20cure_anno%202022.pdf> accessed 22 November 2023.

137 ibid 17.

138 Sandro La Micela, Alessandra Codispoti, Anna Pancheri, Claudia Gadler and Francesca Mulliri, 'La gestione del contenzioso sanitario nell'Azienda Provinciale per i Servizi Sanitari della Provincia Autonoma di Trento a dieci anni dall'introduzione della SIR (self insurance retention) nella polizza di responsabilità civile verso terzi – The Management of Medical Malpractice Litigation in the Provincial Health Care Agency of Trento Ten Years after the Introduction of the SIR (Self Insurance Retention) in the Third Party Liability Insurance Policy' (2023) Riv It Med Leg 235.

139 ibid 246.

filed in 2018 and in 2021 was higher than in 2016 and in 2017, while that of 2020 was lower,[140] and 2022 seems in line with 2017. The average payments decreased from 2017 onwards.[141]

Nonetheless, looking to the loss-ratio of the medical malpractice policies reported by the carriers to IVASS, it can be noticed that – after the Italian reforms – insuring doctors and private hospitals has become profitable, while it remains unprofitable as regards public hospitals.[142]

Mandatory insurance only for practitioners meant new business opportunities for carriers; the availability or at least the affordability of liability insurance for private hospitals has likely improved; however, public hospitals still bear most of the costs of their own medical malpractice, to which the risk of their employees' liability has been added by the legislature.

A hospital study was conducted in Rome after the reforms, looking to malpractice claims for each year in which the accident occurred: between 2014 and 2017 the average was 67; in 2018 the higher result was scored, 77, but claims concerning the following years were considerably less, as the yearly average for the 2018–21 period is 53.[143] However, it is possible that the same hospital will soon receive further claims related to the post-reform period, and if one sums the reported claims with the so-called incurred-but-not-reported claims,[144] s/he may expect that the claims related to injuries occurred in 2018, 2019 and 2020 will be more than the claims concerning injuries occurred in the previous years, while those occurred in 2021 will be lower. Another interesting finding of this study was that only nine claims were brought more than five years after the event.[145]

A study on another hospital in Rome found 567 new claims reported from January 2010 to June 2019, with a decreasing trend from 2015 onwards,[146] which seems thus unrelated to the 2017 reform. Interestingly, 98% of the complaints were filed within seven years of the event.[147]

---

140 ibid 251.
141 ibid 254.
142 IVASS, *Tavole statistiche* (n 111) tab 12.
143 Giuseppe Vetrugno, Federica Foti, Vincenzo M Grassi, Fabio De-Giorgio, Andrea Cambieri, Renato Ghisellini, Francesco Clemente, Luca Marchese, Giuseppe Sabatelli, Giuseppe Delogu, Paola Frati and Vittorio Fineschi, 'Malpractice Claims and Incident Reporting: Two Faces of the Same Coin?' (2022) 19 Int J Environ Res Public Health, 16253, 1, 4–7.
144 ibid 2, 4–7.
145 ibid Tab S1.
146 Raffaele La Russa, Rocco Valerio Viola, Stefano D'Errico, Mariarosaria Aromatario, Aniello Maiese, Paolo Anibaldi, Christian Napoli, Paola Frati, and Vittorio Fineschi, 'Analysis of Inadequacies in Hospital Care through Medical Liability Litigation' (2021) 18 Int J Environ Res Public Health 3425, 1, 3.
147 ibid 3.

An article about a hospital in Terni reported an increase in claims in 2018 compared to the previous year,[148] with an average lag of 28 months between the event and the filing of the claim.[149] As regards the Trento province, around 80% of the 603 claims closed between 2013 and the first semester of 2022 have been managed out-of-court, 2% went to mediation, 11.8% were civil trials and 3.3% were related to criminal proceedings,[150] being thus the criminal trials around three or four times less frequent than in the 1997–2001 period.[151] If the events to which all these studies refer were purported errors committed during the treatment, we could draw some conclusion on the statute of limitations. We already saw that claims against the Italian hospitals can be brought for up to 10 years after the victim perceives or may reasonably perceive the harm as a result of another's intentional or negligent conduct. Accordingly, in addition to the uncertainty on the starting point, this limitation period could be criticised also for being too long given the number of claims made well after the fact. And the same could be said also before the reforms.[152]

As dockets and decisions in Italy are currently, at least theoretically, electronic, searching for medical malpractice decisions and analysing their content should be easier than ever before. A study found that, in 2018, at the court of first instance in Rome, the chamber in charge of medical malpractice

148 Luigi Carlini, Lisa Franceschetto, Sara Gioia, Massimo Lancia and Fabio Suadoni, 'Autoritenzione del Rischio Professionale in Umbria: esperienza dell'Azienda Ospedaliera "Santa Maria" di Terni. Studio di 310 casi – Self-Funded Insurance Risk Management in Umbria: Experience of the St. Mary's Hospital in Terni: Study on 310 Cases' (2019) Riv It Med Leg 1411, 1419.

149 ibid 1417.

150 La Micela, Codispoti, Pancheri, Gadler and Mulliri (n 138) 245–46.

151 Umberto Izzo and Giovanni Pascuzzi (eds), *La responsabilità medica nella Provincia Autonoma di Trento: Il fenomeno. I problemi. Le possibili soluzioni* (Giunta della Provincia Autonoma di Trento 2003) 319–25.

152 Adriano Fileni, Nicola Magnavita, Paoletta Mirk, Ivo Iavicoli, Giulia Magnavita and Antonio Bergamaschi, 'Radiologic Malpractice Litigation Risk in Italy: An Observational Study Over a 14-Year Period' (2010) 194 Am J Roentgenol 1040, 1042; Umberto Tarantino, Alessio Giai Via, Ernesto Macrì, Alessandro Eramo, Valeria Marino and Luigi Tonino Marsella, 'Professional Liability in Orthopaedics and Traumatology in Italy' (2013) 471 Clin Orthop Relat Res 3349, 3352; Regione Emilia-Romagna, *Report Sinistri del Servizio sanitario della Regione Emilia-Romagna Quadriennio 2008–2011 e aggiornamenti 2012* (2014) 45 <https://assr.regione. emilia-romagna.it/pubblicazioni/rapporti-documenti/report-sinistri-ssr-2008-2011-2012/@@ download/publicationFile/report-sinistri-2008-2012.pdf> accessed 14 June 2023; Gian-Aristide Norelli, Federica De Luca, Martina Focardi, Raffaella Giardiello and Vilma Pinchi, 'The Claims Management Committees Trial: Experience of an Italian Hospital of the National Health System' (2015) 29 J Forensic Leg Med 6, 8; Luigi Buzzacchi, Giuseppe Scellato and Elisa Ughetto, 'Frequency of Medical Malpractice Claims: The Effects of Volumes and Specialties' (2016) 170 Soc Sci Med 152, 156, 158.

issued ca 280 decisions,[153] half for the claimants and half for the defendants (mostly hospitals). Moreover, this data indicates the average trial lasted 4.3 years, with proceedings commencing on average 5.3 years after the event. The court rested with the opinions of its appointed experts in 97% of cases.[154] Although in those cases the *legge Gelli-Bianco* was not yet applicable, the aforementioned study is an excellent example for designing possible future research on its application by the Italian courts.

It must be also noted that claimants lost around 18% more cases and the court followed 10% more of its appointed experts' opinions in 2018 than in the 2001–07 period.[155]

An enquiry on some courts in Tuscany found that individual experts, rather than the panels urged by the reform,[156] are still appointed in more than 50% of the trials.[157]

As stated before, statutory provisions on scheduled damages are a special feature of the Italian experience. Some empirical studies on data collected prior to the enactment of the *decreto Balduzzi* and the *legge Gelli-Bianco* found a positive correlation between the inefficiency of courts, their voluntary adoption of scheduled damages and an increase in the availability of insurance (albeit premiums are unaffected).[158] This positive correlation is also related to an increase in the number of unnecessary Caesarean sections in small-sized hospitals.[159]

As discussed, some relevant aspects of substantive law are still in the domain of the judiciary, eg those on the burden of proving causation, which according to recent decisions from the *Cassazione* must be borne by the claimant also in contractual liability cases.[160]

Like in France, there are scholars in Italy, too, who doubt the reliability of information about defensive medicine deriving from surveys,[161] which

153 Michele Treglia, Margherita Pallocci, Pierluigi Passalacqua, Jacopo Giammatteo, Lucilla De Luca, Silvestro Mauriello, Alberto Michele Cisterna and Luigi Tonino Marsella, 'Medical Liability: Review of a Whole Year of Judgments of the Civil Court of Rome' (2021) 18 Int J Environ Res Public Health 6019, 3–4.
154 ibid 5.
155 Corrado Cartoni, 'Il giudice civile e la responsabilità sanitaria' (2013) Giust Civ 531.
156 Art 15, co 1 *legge Gelli-Bianco*.
157 Denise Amram, Giovanni Comandé, Cinzia Della Mora, Lorella Fedeli, Raffaella Giannini, Benedetta Guidi, Isabella Sardella and Andrea Vassallo, 'Responsabilità medica e sanitaria: analisi dei dati dell'azienda sanitaria toscana centro' (2021) Danno e Resp 593, 597.
158 Paola Bertoli and Veronica Grembi, 'Courts, Scheduled Damages, and Medical Malpractice Insurance' (2018) 55 Empir Econ 831.
159 Paola Bertoli and Veronica Grembi, 'Malpractice Risk and Medical Treatment Selection' (2019) 174 J Public Econ 22.
160 Cass civ sez III 14 novembre 2017 n 26824, in Foro It 2018 I, 557ff; Cass civ sez III 26 luglio 2017 n 18392, in Foro It 2017 I, 3358ff.
161 Livio Garattini and Anna Padula, 'Defensive Medicine in Europe: A "Full Circle"?' (2020) 21 Eur J Health Econ 165, 166.

nonetheless are still administered:[162] recently, one also has been conducted on the perception of the *legge Gelli-Bianco* by healthcare professionals.[163]

Conclusions

The current available data related to medical malpractice litigation and insurance after the reforms show some evidence of their effectiveness and efficiency, especially with regard to France and Italy.

Immediately after the French reforms, the costs borne by the companies insuring doctors have likely increased, but they probably decreased by the following decade. Nonetheless, the liability field is still said to be unprofitable, the market is concentrated, and the medical malpractice costs clearly grew at least for the self-insured hospitals in the Paris area.

The *Assistance Publique* receives today more filings than before the reforms, leading mostly to out-of-court procedures, while the number of cases assigned to the administrative tribunals is lower than some past results. The frequency of claims regarding doctors seems to have decreased, but this might be due also to case law rules that predate the French reforms.

However, there is evidence of some effects of the French medical malpractice acts of 2002. Indeed, there has been an increase in the judicial defeats of doctors, which has been explained by the fact that after the *loi Kouchner* the cases of *aléa*, in which criminal and civil courts would have found for the defendants in the past, have been diverted to a no-fault scheme that nowadays allows compensation, so the incidence of good negligence cases tried by the judiciary increased.

An overall decrease in litigation from 2004 to 2006 has been also observed.

The *commissions de conciliation et d'indemnisation* established by the *loi Kouchner* gained a relevant institutional place: they filter many claims, and their opinions enjoy a high confirmation rate by the courts. There are, of course, criticisms and room for improvements. From 2018, the very same

---

162 Vittorio Fineschi, Mauro Arcangeli, Nicola Di Fazio, Zoe Del Fante, Benedetta Fineschi, Paola Santoro and Paola Frati, 'Defensive Medicine in the Management of Cesarean Delivery: A Survey among Italian Physicians' (2021) 9 Healthcare (Basel) 1097; Ismail Zaed, Grazia Menna, Anna Maria Auricchio, Franco Servadei, Diego Garbossa, Alessandro Olivi and Giuseppe Maria Della Pepa, 'Medicolegal Issues: Perception, Awareness, and Behavioral Changes among Italian Neurosurgical Community: Survey-Based Analysis' (2021) 154 World Neurosurgery e774; Pasquale Scognamiglio, Donato Morena, Nicola Di Fazio, Giuseppe Delogu, Valeria Iniziato, Silvestro La Pia, Pasquale Saviano, Paola Frati and Vittorio Fineschi, '*Vox clamantis in deserto*: A Survey among Italian Psychiatrists on Defensive Medicine and Professional Liability' (2023) 14 Front Psychiatry 1244101.

163 Giuseppe Davide Albano, Arianna Rifiorito, Ginevra Malta, Erika Serena Sorrentino, Vincenzo Falco, Alberto Firenze, Antonina Argo and Stefania Zerbo, 'The Impact on Healthcare Workers of Italian Law n. 24/2017 "Gelli – Bianco" on Patient Safety and Medical Liability: A National Survey' (2022) 19 Int J Environ Res Public Health 8448.

commissions receive fewer cases, but it does not seem possible to speak of a crisis of these bodies as no recent data seems available from other institutional players, eg on how many cases are brought to the judiciary or how many claims are made to the insurance companies.

Conversely, the German reform of 2013 did not modify institutional aspects. Thus, it was not able to channel the new disputes towards out-of-court paths, some of which show clear signs of distress. If one confronts the 2013–21 data set from the different German sources, s/he will see filings with the *Schlichtungsstellen* and the *Gutachterkommissionen* are constantly decreasing; the advisory assignments to the MDK peaked in 2016 and then had a less straightforward decrease; the amount of courts' decisions has been more stable.

It is possible to infer a general decrease of medical malpractice litigation in Germany, but there are also signs of increasing awards sought by the claimants and the German liability insurers state an increase in cost of major claims.

For several reasons, the consequences of Italian reform of 2017 are yet to consolidate. However, after the *legge Gelli-Bianco* the Italian liability insurance market is already noticeably more concentrated. Mandatory insurance only for practitioners meant new business opportunities for carriers. The availability or at least the affordability of liability insurance for private hospitals has likely improved. However, public hospitals still bear most of the costs of their own medical malpractice, to which the risk of their employees' liability has been added by the legislature.

The frequency of claims against Italian public hospitals increased since 2017, although it is lower today than in 2015. As regards the costs, the evidence is scarce and mixed: the average payment for damages rose considerably in Lombardia, while decreasing in the Trento province; at a national level, there is data concerning only 2017 and 2018, pointing to a decrease in awards for personal injuries, but also to an increase in those for deaths.

There are some signs that it is more difficult for Italian claimants to prevail in medical malpractice cases and that criminal proceedings might be decreasing.

Even after the aforementioned reforms, some aspects of medical malpractice law still deserve to be addressed by the legislatures of these Civil Law countries in the near future. To this end, comparative law might have something to offer.

In France and Italy, the current starting points of the limitation periods and of the French long-stop allow malpractice claims to be brought an uncertain number of (several) years after the wrongful act, despite most cases are brought shortly after the medical treatment. Only the German legislature has set a maximum period, starting from the act and not from the appearance or consolidation of the injury, which seems capable of meeting the actuarial needs of the insurance industry and of well-designed self-retention systems, which in turn is essential for effective compensation of the victims.

And it could also be argued that even a 10-year long-stop starting from the act (and not from the appearance or consolidation of the injury) would still allow most of the claims to be timely brought.

Empirical legal research on the US reforms showed that the most effective changes in legislation regard damages.[164]

Among the countries analysed, Italy is the only one to have made the use of statutory scheduled damages compulsory in all medical malpractice cases. We also know that the *decreto Balduzzi* and the *legge Gelli-Bianco* require to consider also compliance with clinical practice guidelines, and that at the end of 2023, due to a significant delay in the adoption of a regulation by the Italian government, the schedules still only applied to minor bodily injuries,[165] while for major bodily injuries the courts use other schedules that have been jointly elaborated by judges, lawyers, medico-legal experts and scholars.[166]

Moreover, Italian scholars studying data from the pre-reforms period suggest that scheduled damages may not affect the cost of premiums if courts *per se* do not work properly,[167] and that they may have counter-intuitive impacts on the behaviour of doctors in some hospital settings.[168] The post-reforms evidence on the level of damages paid in Italy is, as stated earlier, scarce and mixed.

Nonetheless, one can argue that scheduled damages offer, at least theoretically, a certain degree of standardisation in the calculation of awards for pain and suffering. Predictability of awards facilitates in turn the functioning of the insurance market, as well as of well-designed self-retention systems, and so enhances the likelihood of compensation. In France, several commentors lamented that a uniform way of quantifying damages is lacking and should be therefore adopted, so the French legislature might benefit from the Italian experience. This seems more difficult for Germany, where courts as of today do not take into consideration the age of the victims, whereas the Italian schedules do.

Finally, some further quantitative research on medical malpractice can be performed in the near future with regard to these countries. A comparative

---

164 Paul C Weiler, *Medical Malpractice on Trial* (Harvard UP 1991) 37.

165 The scheduled damages for *lesioni di lieve entità* (minor bodily injuries), ie up to 9 out 100 points of incapacity, can be inferred by art 139, co 1, lett a and co 6 *Codice delle assicurazioni* (insurance code); the legislature set 1 May 2022 as the deadline for adopting the regulation regarding bodily injuries causing from 10 to 100 points of incapacity, which unfortunately expired.

166 Osservatorio sulla Giustizia Civile di Milano, *Tabelle milanesi per la liquidazione del danno non patrimoniale – Edizione 2021* <www.milanosservatorio.it/wp-content/uploads/2021/03/OSS-MI-TABELLE-2021-LIQUIDAZIONE-DANNO-NON-PATRIMONIALE-ALLA-PERSONA.pdf> accessed 15 September 2023; Cass civ sez III 7 giugno 2011 n 12408, in Foro It 2011 I, 2274.

167 Bertoli and Grembi (n 158).

168 Bertoli and Grembi (n 159).

perspective might be useful, if not for confronting results scored by each country, at least for taking inspiration in designing new studies.

In France and Italy, hospital assistance is largely provided for by public facilities, but all three countries analysed, including Germany, assigned supervisory roles on the healthcare services and on the insurance market to public bodies. These are likely already collecting a lot of data on medical treatments and on subsequent liability claims, or at least they might be interested in improving their knowledge of these phenomena.

Accordingly, French senators and scholars suggested that further information from public bodies be made available to the public and regularly published.[169] The *Allgemeine Ortskrankenkasse* (AOK) and the MDK asked for the creation of a national central database on medical malpractice.[170] Italy already has one in place, but data mining could be further improved, and aggregate information on costs should be made public also with regard to the last years.

Statistics on medical malpractice litigation coming from the German judiciary appear to be a very good reference for other countries who wish to publish their own. France has already showed that it can provide similar data on request,[171] whereas today Italy has at least the informatic infrastructure for trying. In that country, while research on the national features of medical malpractice trials seems yet to come, there are already good examples of studies on the decisions of some courts, which can be easier to perform than in the past.

In France, Germany and Italy there is still room for enhancing research collaborations with insurance companies, which notwithstanding the rise of self-retention systems collect a relevant share of information on medical malpractice. Some of it is already reported by the carriers to public supervisory bodies, but as of today only Italy adopted a transparent approach with regard to this data.

Larger studies, combining data from multiple sources, could follow a French example of scholarship,[172] and they would be very useful for either a first comprehensive analysis or an update on medical malpractice in the aforementioned countries.

---

169 Procaccia (n 13) 18, 23; David Noguéro, 'Rapport conclusif. Le risque médical entre solidarité et assurance. 20 ans après la loi About du 30 décembre 2002' (2023) Resp civ et assur, dossier 25.
170 Ned Stafford, 'German Insurers Call for Central Database of Complaints against Doctors' (2016) 353 BMJ i2815.
171 Thouvenin (n 60); Helmlinger and Martin (n 57); Laude, Pariente and Tabuteau (n 33).
172 Laude, Pariente and Tabuteau (n 33).

Suggested Further Reading List

Taylor S, *Medical Accident Liability and Redress in English and French Law* (CUP 2015)

Treglia M, Pallocci M, Passalacqua P, Giammatteo J, De Luca L, Mauriello S, Cisterna A M and Marsella L T, 'Medical Liability: Review of a Whole Year of Judgments of the Civil Court of Rome' (2021) 18 Int J Environ Res Public Health 6019

Conclusion

Before the age of the reforms, medical malpractice law in France, Germany and Italy exhibited signs of imbalance and unsustainability.

Around the end of the XX century, these countries experienced a surge in medical malpractice litigation. Soaring costs of claims were paired with lower availability of insurance, which might have prevented full achievement of the compensatory objective of medical malpractice law.

Moreover, evidence of an improvement in healthcare deriving from the fear of litigation was almost absent or mixed, so that the deterrent effect of medical malpractice law has failed to materialise. Evidence of defensive medicine too was almost absent or mixed, and while it might complicate matters for claimants' lawyers, it does not lead to better medical treatments.

Faced with these results, France, Germany and Italy adopted statutes in order to reform their medical malpractice laws.

From a comparative law perspective, these acts can first be distinguished according to their general purpose. On the one hand, the German *Patienten-rechtegesetz* was aimed primarily at codifying the solutions already found in case law in order to achieve greater transparency and legal certainty for the victims. On the other hand, the French and Italian statutes had a broader scope and pursued legal innovation, sometimes even repealing case law, as occurred in Italy with the *contatto sociale qualificato* doctrine.

Legal scholars from these countries have proposed adopting broad no-fault systems for medical malpractice, but today only France has such a system in place, and only for serious injuries. Strict liability remains sectoral. On the contrary, there is a general legislative trend towards confirming negligence as the main liability rule for medical malpractice, with the exception of the contractual analysis of the liability of hospitals and independent practitioners in Italy, which involves a lighter burden of proof for the claimant.

Regarding the statute of limitations, France and Germany sought uniformity, while Italy abandoned it by applying the tort analysis to the liability of employed doctors. There are good reasons for both solutions: a single limitation period promotes clarity and equality, while shortening the time limit for actions against employees may lead claimants to focus on the deep pockets of employers (ie hospitals), thus relieving doctors from the pressure of litigation.

DOI: 10.4324/9781003440277-5

However, there is another important distinction to be made. The German *Schuldrechtsmodernisierungsgesetz* links the beginning of its 30-year limitation period to the act, breach of duty or other event that caused the injury. The 10-year limitation period under *loi Kouchner* starts from the consolidation of the injury, which can be a long and uncertain time after the wrongful act, and the same could be said of the 20-year long-stop that has theoretically applied to medical malpractice cases since 2016. The *legge Gelli-Bianco* does not appear to have even considered the fact that, in Italy, case law establishes limitation periods, be they five or 10 years, which do not begin to run until the aggrieved party learns the harm was caused by the intentional or negligent conduct of another, which can be much later than the medical treatment.

As regards damages awards, among the countries analysed herein, Italy is the only one to have made compulsory the use of statutory scheduled damages in all medical malpractice cases, but the *decreto Balduzzi* and the *legge Gelli-Bianco* require to consider also compliance with clinical practice guidelines.

Although the risk of direct liability of employed doctors towards the patients is much lower in France than in Italy, both countries sought to relieve this class of clinicians of the costs of liability insurance, which was made compulsory for all healthcare providers.

This aspect of the reform was promisingly pursued by France, which, unlike Italy, created an underwriting obligation for insurance companies. Both countries allowed hospitals to adopt self-retention mechanisms, thus leaving open the possibility of doing without liability insurance. However, French hospitals must obtain authorisation from the government, which as of today has been granted just to the *Assistance Publique* in the Paris area, whereas Italian hospitals do not have this requirement; this is not to say they do not undergo regulatory guidance, which has been recently adopted. Indeed, mixed systems might not work well if the scope of mandatory insurance and alternative risk retention differ, as such variance incentivises the use of insurance policies by high-risk healthcare providers only.

Changes in civil procedure and in the law of evidence have been limited. The previous Civil Law features of court-appointed experts were confirmed. The German experience of the *Gutachterkommissionen* and of the *Schlichtungsstellen* probably inspired the French reform, while in Italy mandatory mediation or pre-trial court-appointed expert panels have been adopted. Therefore, in the face of long-lasting trials, the general trend is to entrust alternative dispute resolution bodies with the task of speeding up the resolution of medical malpractice disputes, albeit with the risk of creating a kind of parallel justice system.

As regards criminal law, both the French and the Italian legislatures felt the need to set more stringent conviction requirements. However, the *decreto Balduzzi* and the *legge Gelli-Bianco* adopted very complicated formulations, and the scope of the latter has been narrowed by the *Cassazione*, so this aspect of the Italian reform may end up having little impact.

The current available data related to medical malpractice litigation and insurance show some evidence of the effectiveness and efficiency of the reforms, especially with regard to France and Italy.

Immediately after the enactment of French statutes, the costs borne by the companies insuring doctors have likely increased, but they likely lowered almost a decade later. Nonetheless, the liability field is still said to be unprofitable, the market is concentrated, and the medical malpractice costs clearly grew at least for the self-insured hospitals in the Paris area.

The *Assistance Publique* receives today more filings than before the reforms, leading mostly to out-of-court procedures, while the number of cases getting to the administrative tribunals is lower than some results of the past. The frequency of claims regarding doctors seems to have declined, but this might be due also to case law rules that predate the French reforms.

However, there has been an increase in the judicial defeats of doctors, which has been explained with the fact that after the *loi Kouchner* the cases of *aléa thérapeutique*, in which criminal and civil courts would have found for the defendants in the past, have been diverted to a no-fault scheme that nowadays allows compensation, and so the incidence of good negligence cases tried by the judiciary increased.

An overall decrease in litigation from 2004 to 2006 has been also observed.

The *commissions de conciliation et d'indemnisation* established by the *loi Kouchner* gained a relevant institutional place: they filter many claims, and their opinions enjoy a high confirmation rate by the courts. There are, of course, criticisms and room for improvements.

To the contrary, the German reform of 2013 did not modify institutional aspects. Consequently, it was not able to channel the new disputes towards out-of-court paths, some of which show signs of distress indeed. If one confronts the 2013–21 series of data from the different German sources, s/he will see that filings with the *Schlichtungsstellen* and the *Gutachterkommissionen* are constantly decreasing; the advisory assignments to *Medizinische Dienst der Krankenversicherung* peaked in 2016 and then had a less straightforward decrease; the number of courts' decisions has been more stable.

A general diminution of medical malpractice litigation in Germany may be inferred, but there are also signs of increasing awards sought by the claimants, and the German liability insurers state that major claims are getting more expensive.

For several reasons, the consequences of Italian reform of 2017 are yet to consolidate. However, after the *legge Gelli-Bianco* the Italian liability insurance market is noticeably more concentrated. Mandatory insurance only on the side of practitioners meant new business opportunities for carriers. The availability or at least the affordability of liability insurance for private hospitals has likely improved. However, public hospitals still bear most of the costs of their own medical malpractice, to which the risk of their employees' liability has been added by the legislature.

The frequency of claims against Italian public hospitals increased since 2017, although it is lower today than in 2015. As regards the costs, the evidence is scarce and mixed.

There are some signs that medical malpractice cases have become more difficult to win for the Italian claimants and that criminal proceedings might be decreasing.

Even after the aforementioned reforms, some aspects of medical malpractice law still deserve to be addressed by the legislatures of these Civil Law countries in the near future. To this end, comparative law might have something to offer.

First, the statutes of limitation can be improved in France and Italy, and from this respect they might look to the German experience, where the solutions adopted seem to meet the actuarial needs of the insurance industry and of well-designed self-retention systems, which in turn is essential for effective compensation of the victims.

Secondly, as regards compensation, scheduled damages aim, theoretically, at a higher degree of standardisation in the calculation of awards for pain and suffering. Predictability of awards facilitates in turn the functioning of the insurance market, and also of well-designed self-retention systems, thus enhancing the likelihood of compensation. In France, several commentors lamented that a uniform way of quantifying damages is lacking and should be therefore adopted, so the French legislature might benefit from the Italian experience. This seems more difficult for Germany, where courts as of today do not take into consideration the age of the victims, whereas the Italian schedules do.

Finally, some further quantitative research on medical malpractice can be performed in the near future with regard to these countries. A comparative perspective might be useful, if not for confronting results scored by each country, at least for taking inspiration in designing new studies.

All three countries analysed assigned supervisory roles to the healthcare services and to the insurance market to public bodies. These are likely already collecting a lot of data on medical treatments and subsequent liability claims. Or at least they might be interested in improving their knowledge of these phenomena. Information from public bodies should therefore be regularly published and made available to the public. National central data collections on medical malpractice could be set up, as already happened in Italy, where nonetheless data mining could be further improved and aggregate information on costs should be made public also with regard to the last years.

Statistics on medical malpractice litigation coming from the German judiciary seem a very good reference for other countries that wanted to publish their own. France has already showed that it can provide similar data on request, whereas today Italy has at least the digital infrastructure to try. In that country, while research on the national features of medical malpractice trials seems yet to come, there are already good examples of studies on the decisions of some courts, which may be more easily performed than in the past.

In France, Germany and Italy there is still room for improving research collaborations with insurance companies, which notwithstanding the rise of self-retention systems collect a relevant share of information on medical malpractice. Some of it is already reported by the carriers to public supervisory bodies, but as of today only Italy has adopted a transparent approach with regard to this data.

Larger studies, combining data from multiple sources, could follow a French example of scholarship, and they would be very useful for either a first comprehensive analysis or an update on medical malpractice in the aforementioned countries.

Bibliography

———, *Audition de M. Bernard Kouchner, ministre délégué à la santé, sur le projet de loi relatif aux droits des malades et la qualité du système de santé – n° 3258 (MM. Claude Evin, Jean-Jacques Denis, Bernard Charles, rapporteurs)* <www.assemblee-nationale.fr/11/cr-cafc/00-01/c0001049. asp> accessed 28 August 2023

———, 'French Obstetricians Strike' (2003) 326 BMJ 68

Abel R L, 'Real Tort Crisis – Too Few Claims' (1987) 48 Ohio St LJ 443

Adida-Canac H, 'Le contrôle de la nomenclature Dintilhac par la Cour de cassation' (2011) D 1497

Albano G D, Rifiorito A, Malta G, Sorrentino E S, Falco V, Firenze A, Argo A and Zerbo S, 'The Impact on Healthcare Workers of Italian Law n. 24/2017 "Gelli – Bianco" on Patient Safety and Medical Liability: A National Survey' (2022) 19 Int J Environ Res Public Health 8448

Alpa G, 'Ars interpretandi e responsabilità sanitaria a seguito della nuova legge Bianco-Gelli' (2017) Contr Impr 728

Amaral-Garcia S, Bertoli P and Grembi V, 'Does Experience Rating Improve Obstetric Practices? Evidence from Italy' (2015) 24 Health Econ 1050

Amaral-Garcia S and Grembi V, 'Economia della malpractice medica', in Franzoni M (ed), *La responsabilità nei servizi sanitari* (Zanichelli 2011)

———, 'Curb Your Premium: The Impact of Monitoring Malpractice Claims' (2014) 114 Health Policy 139

Amodio C, 'La responsabilità medica nell'esperienza francese: profili comparatistici' (2002) Contr Impr Eur 528

Amram D, Comandé G, Della Mora C, Fedeli L, Giannini R, Guidi B, Sardella I and Vassallo A, 'Responsabilità medica e sanitaria: analisi dei dati dell'azienda sanitaria toscana centro' (2021) Danno e Resp 593

Aprile A, Bolcato M, Fabbri L D, Pagan S and Rodriguez D, 'Analisi e valutazione medico-legale di 1004 casi di responsabilità professionale in ambito sanitario' (2013) Riv It Med Leg 93

Assistance Publique – Hôpitaux de Paris, *Responsabilité médicale. Bilan de l'année 2014* <https://cme.aphp.fr/sites/default/files/CMEDoc/bilanre sponsabilitemedicale2014.pdf> accessed 20 September 2023

———, 'Responsabilité médicale', *Bilan de l'année 2016* (2017) <https:// cme.aphp.fr/sites/default/files/CMEDoc/cme7novembre2017_responsabil itemedicale_bilan.pdf> accessed 20 September 2023

Associazione Nazionale fra le Imprese Assicuratrici (ANIA), *Italian Insurance 2012–2013* (2013) <www.ania.it/documents/35135/126704/Italian-Insurance-in-2012-2013.pdf/4f2ef508-2dbc-131e-7c40-25cb9e330132?version=1.0&t=1575554686678> accessed 12 June 2023
———, *L'assicurazione italiana 2012–2013* (2013) <https://ania.it/documents/35135/0/Assicurazione-Italiana-2012-2013.pdf/1a921ad3-efd4-6073-50f3-7c05a5770b0b?t=1576519512151> accessed 12 June 2023
Auby J-M, 'La responsabilité médicale en France (aspects de droit public)' (1976) 28 Rev Intern Dr Comp 511
Bach-Golecka D, 'Compensation Schemes and Extra-Judicial Solutions in Case of Medical Malpractice: A Commentary on Contemporary Arrangements', in Boele-Woelki K, Fernández Arroyo D P and Senegacnik A (eds), *General Reports of the XXth General Congress of the International Academy of Comparative Law* (Springer 2020)
Baker T, *The Medical Malpractice Myth* (Chicago UP 2005)
Barbot J and Fillion J, 'La "médecine défensive": critique d'un concept à succès' (2006) 24(2) Sci soc santé 5
Barbot J, Parizot I and Winancea M, '"No-Fault" Compensation for Victims of Medical Injuries: Ten Years of Implementing the French Model' (2014) Health Policy 263
Basile F and Poli P F, 'La responsabilità per "colpa medica" a cinque anni dalla legge Gelli-Bianco – Responsibility for "Medical Malpractice" Five Years after the Gelli-Bianco Law' (2022) (1) Dir Pen Cont Riv Trim 79
Bercot R and Mathieu-Fritz A, 'La crise de recrutement des chirurgiens français: entre mythes et réalités' (2007) 48 Revue française de sociologie 751
Bergmann K O and Wever C, *Die Arzthaftung: Ein Leitfaden für Ärzte und Juristen* (4th edn, Springer 2014)
Bernardinangeli C, Giannace C, Cerciello S, Grassi V M, Lodise M, Vetrugno G and De-Giorgio F, 'A Fifteen-Year Survey for Orthopedic Malpractice Claims in the Criminal Court of Rome' (2023) 11 Healthcare 962
Bert D, 'Feu l'arrêt Mercier!' (2010) D 1801
Bertoli P and Grembi V, 'Courts, Scheduled Damages, and Medical Malpractice Insurance' (2018) 55 Empir Econ 831
———, 'Malpractice Risk and Medical Treatment Selection' (2019) 174 J Public Econ 22
Blancher G, 'Faut-il dépénaliser la responsabilité médicale?' (2001) 185 Bulletin de l'Académie nationale de médecine 1717
Bonetti M, Cirillo P, Musile Tanzi P and Trinchero E, 'An Analysis of the Number of Medical Malpractice Claims and Their Amounts' (2016) 11 PloS One 1 <https://doi.org/10.1371/journal.pone.0153362> accessed 26 May 2023
Borghetti J-S, 'France', in Gilead I and Askeland B (eds), *Prescription in Tort Law: Analytical and Comparative Perspectives* (Intersentia 2020)
Boutonnet M, Trouiller P, Lopard E, Amalberti R, Houselstein T, Pasquier P, Auroy Y and De Saint-Maurice G, 'Insurance Statements from French Anaesthesiologists and Intensivists: A Database Analysis' (2016) 35 Anaesth Crit Care Pain Med 313

Bras P-L, d'Autume C, Roussille B and Saintoyant V, *L'assurance en responsabilité civile médicale* (2007) <https://medias.vie-publique.fr/data_storage_s3/rapport/pdf/074000243.pdf> accessed 9 November 2023

Brilla R, Evers S, Deutschlander A and Wartenberg K E. 'Are Neurology Residents in the United States being Taught Defensive Medicine?' (2006) 108 Clin Neurol Neurosurg 374

Brun P and Gout O, 'Responsabilité civile' (2015) D 124

Bundesärztekammer, *Statistische Erhebung der Gutachterkommissionen und Schlichtungsstellen: Statistikjahr 2006* <www.aerztekammern-schlichten. de/fileadmin/user_upload/_old-files/downloads/Gutachterkommission_Statistik_2006.pdf> accessed 21 July 2023

Bundesärztekammer und kassenärztliche Bundesvereinigung, *Qualitätssicherung und kontinuierliche Qualitätsverbesserung: Grundlagen einer bedarfsgerechten Gesundheitsversorgung. Gemeinsame Bestandsaufnahme der Bundesärztekammer und der Kassenärztlichen Bundesvereinigung über die Aktivitäten der Spitzenorganisationen der ärztlichen Selbstverwaltung auf dem Gebiet der Qualitätssicherung in der Medizin 1955 bis 1995* (1996) <www.aezq.de/mdb/edocs/pdf/stellungnahmen/sn-qualitaetssicherung-1996.pdf> accessed 24 July 2023

Bundesministerium für Gesundheit, *Statistik über Versicherte, gegliedert nach Status, Alter, Wohnort und Kassenart* (2006) <www.bundesgesund heitsministerium.de/fileadmin/Dateien/3_Downloads/Statistiken/GKV/ Mitglieder_Versicherte/KM6_2006.xls> accessed 14 July 2023

Bundesministerium für Gesundheit und Soziale Sicherung, *Unterrichtung durch die Bundesregierung. Gutachten 2003 des Sachverständigenrates für die Konzertierte Aktion im Gesundheitswesen: Finanzierung, Nutzerorientierung und Qualität* (2003) <https://dserver.bundestag.de/btd/15/005/1500530. pdf> accessed 24 July 2023

Buzzacchi L, Scellato G and Ughetto E, 'Frequency of Medical Malpractice Claims: The Effects of Volumes and Specialties' (2016) 170 Soc Sci Med 152

California Medical Association, *Medical Insurance Feasibility Study* (Sutter Publications 1977)

Carlini L, Franceschetto L, Gioia S, Lancia M and Suadoni F, 'Autoritenzione del Rischio Professionale in Umbria: esperienza dell'Azienda Ospedaliera "Santa Maria" di Terni. Studio di 310 casi – Self-Funded Insurance Risk Management in Umbria: Experience of the St. Mary's Hospital in Terni. Study on 310 Cases' (2019) Riv It Med Leg 1411

Cartoni C, 'Il giudice civile e la responsabilità sanitaria' (2013) Giust Civ 531

Casali M B, Mobilia F, Del Sordo S, Blandino A and Genovese U, 'The Medical Malpractice in Milan-Italy: A Retrospective Survey on 14 Years of Judicial Autopsies' (2014) 242 Forensic Sci Int 38

Castronovo C, 'L'obbligazione senza prestazione ai confini tra contratto e torto', in *Le ragioni del diritto: Scritti in onore di Luigi Mengoni I* (Giuffrè 1995)

Catino M, 'Blame Culture and Defensive Medicine' (2009) 11 Cogn Tech Work 245

Catino M, Pesenti Campagnoni M and Locatelli C, 'La medicina difensiva: una ricerca sul Pronto Soccorso in Italia' (2011) 5 Pratica Medica & Aspetti Legali 35

Ceretti A-M and Albertini L, *Bilan et propositions de réformes de la loi du 4 mars 2002 relative aux droits des malades et à la qualité du système de santé* (2011) <www.vie-publique.fr/rapport/31615-bilan-et-propositions-de-reformes-de-la-loi-du-4-mars-2002-relative-aux> accessed 9 November 2023

Claudot F, Allac F, Villemot J-P, Aliot E, Coudanea H and Juillière Y, 'Analysis of Patient Claims Related to Care in a University Cardiology Department Over the Period 2003–2007' (2010) 103 Arch Cardiovasc Dis 595

Coggiola N, 'Medical Liability Law in Italy' (2019) 23 Journal du Droit de la Santé et de l'Assurance - Maladie 45

Colaianni P, 'Autoassicurazione e assicurazione nella responsabilità civile medica', in Landini S (ed), *Autoassicurazione e gestione del rischio* (CESIFIN 2015) <www.cesifin.it/wp-content/uploads/2016/12/AUTO ASSICURAZIONE_E_GESTIONE_DEL_RISCHIO_22_09_15.pdf> accessed 6 October 2023

Comandé G, 'Dalla responsabilità sanitaria al no-blame regionale tra conciliazione e risarcimento' (2010) Danno e Resp 977

———, 'La responsabilità sanitaria al tempo del coronavirus ... e dopo' (2020) Danno e Resp 297

Commission des Affaires Sociales, *Rapport fait au nom de la Commission des Affaires Sociales sur le projet de loi relatif à la santé, par m. Olivier Véran, mme Bernadette Laclais, m. Jean-Louis Touraine, mme Hélène Geoffroy et m. Richard Ferrand* <www.assemblee-nationale.fr/14/rapports/r2673.asp> accessed 15 September 2023

Commission nationale des accidents médicaux (CNAMed), *Rapport annuel au parlement et au gouvernement année 2013* <https://sante.gouv.fr/IMG/pdf/CNAMed2013.pdf> accessed 10 November 2023

Conen D, Gerlach F, Grandt D, Hart D, Jonitz G, Lauterberg J, Lessing C, Loskill H, Rothmund M and Schrappe M, *Agenda Patientensicherheit 2006* (Aktionsbündnis Patientensicherheit e.V. 2006) <http://schrappe.com/ms2/index_htm_files/agenda2006.pdf> accessed 27 July 2023

Cour des comptes, *L'indemnisation amiable des victimes d'accidents médicaux: une mise en œuvre dévoyée, une remise en ordre impérative* (2017) <www.ccomptes.fr/sites/default/files/EzPublish/02-indemnisation-amiable-accidents-medicaux-Tome-1.pdf> accessed 10 November 2023

Cupelli C, 'Art 590-Sexies c p', in Dolcini E and Gatta G L (eds), *Codice penale commentato* (5th edn, Wolters Kluwer 2021)

Danzon P, *Medical Malpractice: Theory, Evidence, and Public Policy* (HUP 1985)

———, 'The Crisis in Medical Malpractice: A Comparison of Trends in the United States, Canada, the United Kingdom and Australia' (1990) 18 L Med & Health Care 48

Darchy B, Le Mière E, Figueredo B, Bavoux E and Domart Y, 'Iatrogenic Diseases as a Reason for Admission to the Intensive Care Unit: Incidence, Causes, and Consequences' (1999) 159 Arch Intern Med 71

Debono B, Gerson C, Houselstein T, Lettat-Ouatah L, Bougeard R and Lonjon N, 'Litigations Following Spinal Neurosurgery in France: "Out-of-Court System," Therapeutic Hazard, and Welfare State' (2020) 49(5) Neurosurg

Focus E11 <https://doi.org/10.3171/2020.8.FOCUS20582> accessed 20 September 2023

Debono B, Hamel O, Guillain A, Durand A, Rué M, Sabatier P, Lonjon G and Drang G, on behalf of French Society of Private Neurosurgeons (SFNCL), 'Impact of Malpractice Liability among Spine Surgeons: A National Survey of French Private Neurosurgeons' (2020) 66 Neurochirurgie 219

Decroix G, 'Responsabilité médicale en France: mythes et réalité', (2000) 32 ADSP 48 <www.hcsp.fr/Explore.cgi/Telecharger?NomFichier=ad324853. pdf> accessed 4 July 2023

De Lorenzi V, 'Obbligazioni di mezzi e obbligazioni di risultato', *Digesto delle discipline privatistiche: Sezione civile*, vol 12 (1995)

De Matteis R, *La responsabilità medica: Un sottosistema della responsabilità civile* (Cedam 1995)

Demogue R, *Traité des obligations en general V* (Librairie Arthur Rousseau 1925)

Department of Health, *Claims of Medical Negligence Against N.H.S. Hospital and Community Doctors and Dentists*, HC (89) 34

———, *NHS Indemnity: Arrangements for Clinical Negligence Claims in the NHS*, HSG 96/48

Desantis S and Giuli G (eds), *ANIA Trends: Focus R.C. sanità* (2017) <www. ania.it/documents/35135/53795/Ania-Trends-Focus-RC-Sanitaria.pdf/ 6a0f70f9-90cf-2572-aca8-4ceed26f7bab?version=1.0&t=1573729011189> accessed 12 June 2023

Deutsch E and Spickhoff A, *Medizinrecht* (7th edn, Springer 2014)

Dewees D N, Trebilcock M J and Coyte P C, 'The Medical Malpractice Crisis: A Comparative Empirical Perspective' (1991) 54 LCP 217

Didier M and Taubert P, 'Conjoncture de l'assurance et cycle économique', (1998) 33 Risques 33 <www.revue-risques.fr/wp-content/uploads/2019/04/ Risques-033_Web.pdf> accessed 5 July 2023

Di Lella F, 'Leges artis e responsabilità civile sanitaria' (2018) Nuova Giur Civ Comm II 264

Dintilhac J-P, *Rapport du groupe de travail chargé d'élaborer une nomen- clature des préjudices corporels* (2005) <https://sante.gouv.fr/IMG/pdf/ Rapport_groupe_de_travail_nomenclature_des_prejudices_corporels_de_ Jean-Pierre_Dintilhac.pdf> accessed 14 November 2023

Di Nunno N, Dell'Erba A, Viola L, Vimercati L, Cina S and Vimercati F, 'Medical Malpractice: A Study of Case Histories by the Forensic Medicine Section of Bari' (2004) 25 Am J Forensic Med Pathol 141

Donaldson L, *Making Amends: A Consultation Paper Setting Out Proposals for Reforming the Approach to Clinical Negligence in the NHS – A Report by the Chief Medical Officer* (Department of Health Publications 2003)

Durand-Zaleski I, Moreau J-F, Conge E and Blum-Boisgard C, 'Medical Mal- practice in France: The Effects of a Two-Fold Jurisdiction and the Case of Radiology' (1993) 28 Inves Radiol 459

Dwyer D, 'The Role of the Expert under CPR Pt 35', in Dwyer D (ed), *The Civil Procedure Rules Ten Years On* (OUP 2009)

Eissler M, 'Die Ergebnisse der Gutachterkommissionen und Schlichtungss- tellen in Deutschland – Ein bundesweiter Vergleich' (2005) 23 MedR 280

Elli L, Tenca A, Soncini M, Spinzi G, Buscarini E and Conte D, 'Defensive Medicine Practices among Gastroenterologists in Lombardy: Between Lawsuits and the Economic Crisis' (2013) 45 Dig Liver Dis 469

Evin C, Charles B and Denis J-J, *Rapport d'information de MM. Claude Evin, Bernard Charles et Jean-Jacques Denis, déposé en application de l'article 145 du règlement par la commission des aff aires culturelles, sur la loi n° 2002–303 du 4 mars 2002 relative aux droits des malades et à la qualité du système de santé (n° 3688, 11 avril 2002)* <www.assemblee-nationale.fr/11/rap-info/i3688.asp> accessed 28 August 2023

Ewald F and Margeat H, 'Le risque thérapeutique' (1991) 6 Risques 9 <www.revue-risques.fr/wp-content/uploads/Risques-006_Web.pdf> accessed 4 July 2023

Farrell A-M and Devaney S, 'Making Amends or Making Things Worse? Clinical Negligence Reform and Patient Redress in England' (2007) 27 LS 630

Fileni A, Magnavita N, Mammi F, Mandoliti G, Lucà F, Magnavita G and Bergamaschi A, 'Malpractice Stress Syndrome in Radiologists and Radiotherapists: Perceived Causes and Consequences' (2007) 112 Radiologia medica 1069

Fileni A, Magnavita N, Mirk P, Iavicoli I, Magnavita G and Bergamaschi A, 'Radiologic Malpractice Litigation Risk in Italy: An Observational Study Over a 14-Year Period' (2010) 194 AJR 1040

Fineschi V, Arcangeli M, Di Fazio N, Del Fante Z, Fineschi B, Santoro P and Frati P, 'Defensive Medicine in the Management of Cesarean Delivery: A Survey among Italian Physicians' (2021) 9 Healthcare (Basel) 1097

Finocchiaro Castroa M, Lorenzo Ferrara P, Guccio C and Lisi D, 'Medical Malpractice Liability and Physicians' Behavior: Experimental Evidence' (2019) 166 J Econ Behav Organ 646

Fiori A, Bottone E and D'Alessandro E, *Quarant'anni di giurisprudenza della cassazione nella responsabilità medica* (Giuffrè 2000)

Flatscher-Thöni M, Leiter A M and Winner H, 'Are Pain and Suffering Awards (Un-)predictable? Evidence from Germany' (2015) *Working Papers in Economics and Finance University of Salzburg*, No. 2015–02 <http://hdl.handle.net/10419/122168> accessed 15 November 2023

Flintrop J and Korzilius H, 'Arzthaftpflicht: Der Schutz wird teurer' (2010) 107 Dtsch Ärztebl A-692

Forti G, Catino M, D'Alessandro F, Mazzuccato C and Varraso G (eds), *Il problema della medicina difensiva* (Edizioni ETS 2010)

Fortis E, 'La nouvelle définition des délits non intentionnels par la loi du 10 juillet 2000' (2001) RSC 737

Gambaro A, 'Azione civile e processo penale. Appunti di diritto comparato' (1977) Resp Civ Prev 387

———, 'Nuovi spunti in tema di responsabilità sanitaria nella prospettiva comparatistica', in *La responsabilità in materia sanitaria. Atti del Convegno nazionale tenuto a Bologna il 16 dicembre e a Ravenna il 17 dicembre 1983* (Giuffrè 1984)

———, 'Francia', *Digesto delle discipline privatistiche: Sezione civile*, vol 8 (1992)

Garattini L and Padula A, 'Defensive Medicine in Europe: A "Full Circle"?' (2020) 21 Eur J Health Econ 165

Giusti E, 'Assicurazione sanitaria: la legge Balduzzi dopo il d.l. n. 90 del 2014 e alcune riflessioni sul modello autoassicurativo', *Giustiziacivile.com* (5 November 2014) <https://giustiziacivile.com/pdfpage/443> accessed 9 June 2023

Glanzmann P, 'Schlichtungsstellen und Gutachterkommissionen für Fragen ärztlicher Haftpflicht' (2021) 50 Orthopäde 159

Granelli C, 'La riforma della disciplina della responsabilità sanitaria: chi vince e chi perde?' (2017) Contratti 377

Gravot B, Pottie J C, Laxenaire M C, Feldman L, Virion J M and Legras B, 'Evénements indésirables liés à l'anesthésie. Etude prospective d'un an d'activité' (1995) 14 Ann Fr Anesth Réanim R217

Grembi V and Garoupa N, 'Delays in Medical Malpractice Litigation in Civil Law Jurisdictions: Some Evidence from the Italian Court of Cassation' (2013) 8 Health Econ Policy Law 423

Gromb S, 'Responsabilité médicale: va-t-on indemniser l'accident mèdical?' (1996) 16 Médecine & Droit 12

Grossholz C, 'Hôpitaux: régimes de responsabilité et de solidarité', *Répertoire de la responsabilité de la puissance publique Dalloz*, Février 2018 (actualisation: Février 2023) <www-dalloz-fr> accessed 2 May 2023

Ham C, Dingwall R, Fenn P and Harris D, *Medical Negligence: Compensation and Accountability* (King's Fund Institute 1988)

Hansis M L and Hart D, 'Medizinische Behandlungsfehler in Deutschland', *Gesundheitsberichterstattung des Bundes* (4 January 2001) <https://edoc.rki.de/bitstream/handle/176904/3154/24d1rmXbF2ZqM_68.pdf?sequence=1&isAllowed=y> accessed 20 July 2023

Harichaux M, 'L'obligation du médecin de respecter les données de la science (A propos du cinquantenaire de l'arrêt Mercier: bilan d'une jurisprudence)' (1987) JCP G I 3306

Harper R F (tr), *The Code of Hammurabi* (U of Chicago P 1904)

Harvard Medical Practice Study Group, *Patients, Doctors, and Lawyers: Medical Injury, Malpractice Litigation and Patient Compensation in New York* (President and Fellows of Harvard College 1990)

Health and Social Care Committee, *NHS litigation reform: Thirteenth Report of Session 2021–22* (House of Commons 2022) <https://publications.parliament.uk/pa/cm5802/cmselect/cmhealth/740/report.html#heading-5> accessed 28 June 2023

Heberer J and Eicher M, 'Schadenmanagement aus Sicht des Juristen. Top 7 der Fehler im Arzthaftungsrecht' (2020) 123 Der Unfallchirurg 6

Hellberg N and Lonsing M, 'Dramatische Teuerung von Personenschäden im Heilwesen' (2010) VW 421

Helmlinger L and Martin D, 'La judiciarisation de la médecine, mythe et réalité' (2004) 5 Les Tribunes de la santé 39

Herrmann J, 'The Rule of Compulsory Prosecution and the Scope of Prosecutorial Discretion in Germany' (1973) 41 UChLRev 468

Herzog H, 'Zwischen Budget und Haftung – Faktische Rationalisierungsentscheidungen auf dem Rücken der Ärzte' (2007) GesR 8

Holger T, 'Behandlungsfehler und Risikomanagement im AOK-Institut Medizinschaden' (2006) 16 Rechtsmedizin 361, 363–64

Hondius E (ed), *The Development of Medical Liability* (CUP 2010)
Inspection générale des finances and Inspection générale des affaires sociales, *Conclusions du rapport d'enquête sur l'assurance de responsabilite civile medicale* (2004) <https://medias.vie-publique.fr/data_storage_s3/rapport/pdf/044000073.pdf> accessed 26 June 2023
Introna F, 'L'epidemiologia del contenzioso per responsabilità medica in Italia ed all'estero' (1996) Riv It Med Leg 71
———, 'È possible introdurre l'assicurazione obbligatoria per responsabilità professionale medica?' (1997) Riv It Med Leg 1121
Istituto per la Vigilanza sulle Assicurazioni (IVASS), *Report on the activities pursued by IVASS in the year 2014* (2015) <www.ivass.it/pubblicazioni-e-statistiche/pubblicazioni/relazione-annuale/2015/RELAZIONE_IVASS_2014_en.pdf?language_id=3> accessed 29 December 2023
———, 'Healthcare liability risks in Italy 2010–2016' (2017) 4(14) Stat Bull <www.ivass.it/pubblicazioni-e-statistiche/statistiche/bollettino-statistico/2017/n14/report_italian_medmal_2017.pdf?language_id=3> accessed 29 December 2023
———, *Tavole statistiche r.c. sanitaria 2010–2016* (2017) <www.ivass.it/pubblicazioni-e-statistiche/statistiche/bollettino-statistico/2017/n14/RC_SANITARIA.XLSB?force_download=1> accessed 13 June 2023
———, 'I rischi da responsabilità civile generale e sanitaria in Italia' (2022) 14 Bollettino Statistico <www.ivass.it/pubblicazioni-e-statistiche/statistiche/bollettino-statistico/2022/n_14_2022/Bollettino_rcg_rcsanitaria.pdf> accessed 20 November 2023
———, *Tavole statistiche – r.c. sanitaria* (2022) <www.ivass.it/pubblicazioni-e-statistiche/statistiche/bollettino-statistico/2022/n_14_2022/Allegato_B_RC_SANITARIA.xlsb> accessed 20 November 2023
Izzo U, 'Responsabilità sanitaria e Covid-19: scenari di una possibile pandemia giudiziaria e risposte per prevenirla – I parte' (2020) Resp Civ Prev 1768
Izzo U and Pascuzzi G (eds), *La responsabilità medica nella Provincia Autonoma di Trento: Il fenomeno. I problemi. Le possibili soluzioni* (Giunta della Provincia Autonoma di Trento 2003)
Johanet G, *L'assurance responsabilité civile des professionnels de santé* (2011) <https://medias.vie-publique.fr/data_storage_s3/rapport/pdf/114000101.pdf> accessed 9 November 2023
Jourdain P, 'Prescription de l'action en responsabilité extra-contractuelle: en cas de dommage corporel, le délai de la prescription court du jour de la consolidation' (2000) RTDCiv 851
Katzenmeier C, 'Patientenrechtegesetz 2.0? – Haftungsrecht' (2023) 41 MedR 118
Kazarian M, Griffiths D and Brazier M, 'Criminal Responsibility for Medical Malpractice in France' (2011) 27(4) PN 188
Kieker J, 'Patientenrechtegesetz 2.0 aus der Sicht eines Schadenversicherers' (2023) 41 MedR 101
Kirchner R and Lemke R, 'Behandlungsfehlerbegutachtung beim MDK Niedersachsen' (2008) 102 ZEFQ 555
Knaak J-P and Parzeller M, 'Court Decisions on Medical Malpractice' (2014) 128 Int J Legal Med 1049
Knetsch J, 'La désintégration du préjudice moral' (2015) D 443

————, 'The French Medical Accident Compensation Scheme. A Critical Assessment of the Patients' Rights Act of 4 March 2002', in Bach-Golecka D (ed), *Compensation Schemes for Damages Caused by Healthcare and Alternatives to Court Proceedings: Comparative Law Perspectives* (Springer 2021)

Koch B E (ed), *Medical Liability in Europe: A Comparison of Selected Jurisdictions* (De Gruyter 2011)

Kölbel R, 'StPO § 170', Rn. 21–22, in Knauer C, Kudlich H and Schneider H (eds), *Münchener Kommentar zur StPO* (Beck 2016)

Kothe-Pawel G, 'Die Erfolgsaussichten von Klagen in Arzthaftungsprozessen anhand der Ergebnisse vor dem Landgericht Dortmund im Jahr 2009' (2010) 28 MedR 537

Krumpaszky H G, Sethe R and Selbmann H-K, 'Die Häufigkeit von Behandlungsfehlervorwürfen in der Medizin' (1997) 48 VersR 420

La Micela S, Codispoti A, Pancheri A, Gadler C and Mulliri F, 'La gestione del contenzioso sanitario nell'Azienda Provinciale per i Servizi Sanitari della Provincia Autonoma di Trento a dieci anni dall'introduzione della SIR (Self Insurance Retention) nella polizza di responsabilità civile verso terzi – The Management of Medical Malpractice Litigation in the Provincial Health Care Agency of Trento Ten Years after the Introduction of the SIR (Self Insurance Retention) in the Third Party Liability Insurance Policy' (2023) Riv It Med Leg 235

La Russa R, Viola R V, D'Errico S, Aromatario M, Maiese A, Anibaldi P, Napoli C, Frati P and Fineschi V, 'Analysis of Inadequacies in Hospital Care through Medical Liability Litigation' (2021) 18 Int J Environ Res Public Health 3425

Lagnaoui R, Moore N, Fach J, Longy-Boursier M and Bégaud B, 'Adverse Drug Reactions in a Department of Systemic Diseases-Oriented Internal Medicine: Prevalence, Incidence, Direct Costs and Avoidability' (2000) 56 Eur J Clin Pharmacol 181

Lambert-Faivre Y, 'L'éthique de la responsabilité' (1998) RTDCiv 1

Lantero C, 'Responsabilité hospitalière: les articulations entre procédure amiable et procédure contentieuse' (2019) AJDA 2391

————, 'Les consolidations du droit de la responsabilité hospitalière' (2020) AJDA 714

Laude A, Pariente J and Tabuteau D, *La judiciarisation de la santé* (Éditions de Santé 2012)

Le Clainche C and Poquet G, *La responsabilité médicale et l'indemnisation du risque thérapeutique: Etat des lieux* (Centre de Recherche pour l'Étude et l'Observation des Conditions de Vie – CRÉDOC 1992) <www.credoc.fr/download/pdf/Rapp/R128.pdf> accessed 4 July 2023

Lefeuvre A, 'De la prescription décennale en matière de responsabilité médicale' (2003) AJDA 270

Léger A, Manaouil C, Montpellier D, Moquet-Anger M-L and Pierre P, 'Responsabilité médicale et expertise: de la loi du Talion à la loi Kouchner' (2023) 2023 Méd Droit 7

Leleu T, 'Vers la création d'un géant de l'indemnisation: à propos du rapport IGF/IGAS proposant la fusion de l'ONIAM et du FIVA' (2020) Resp civ et assur, étude 12

Levasseur A, 'Les transactions: l'exemple de l'Assistance publique-Hôpitaux de Paris' (1997) AJDA 54

Lonsing M and Hellberg N, 'Superimposed Inflation hält an' (2022) VW 66

Madea B and Doberentz E, 'Häufigkeit letaler Behandlungsfehler in deutschen Kliniken' (2015) 25 Rechtsmedizin 179

Madea B and Preuß J, 'Medical Malpractice as Reflected by the Forensic Evaluation of 4450 Autopsies' (2009) 190 Forensic Sci Int 58

Madea B, Vennedey C, Dettmeyer R and Preuß J, 'Ausgang strafrechtlicher Ermittlungsverfahren gegen Ärzte wegen Verdachts eines Behandlungsfehlers' (2006) 131 DMW 2073

Manca R, Bruti V, Napoletano S and Marinelli E, 'A 15 Years Survey for Dental Malpractice Claims in Rome, Italy' (2018) 58 J Forensic Leg Med 74

Masieri C, 'La responsabilità civile dell'"esercente la professione sanitaria"' (2015) 4 Ricerche Giuridiche 103

———, 'Novità in tema di responsabilita' sanitaria' (2017) Nuova Giur Civ Comm 752

———, *Linee guida e responsabilità civile del medico. Dall'esperienza americana alla legge Gelli-Bianco* (Giuffrè Francis Lefebvre 2019)

———, 'Emergenza pandemica e (ir)responsabilità sanitaria' (2022) Resp Civ Prev 1304

McGrath C P, *The Development of Medical Liability in Germany, 1800–1945* (Vittorio Klostermann 2019)

Medizinischer Dienst Bund and Medizinischer Dienst Bayern, *Jahresstatistik 2018. Behandlungsfehler-Begutachtung der MDK-Gemeinschaft* (2019) <https://md-bund.de/fileadmin/dokumente/Pressemitteilungen/2019/2019_05_16/2019-08-12_Behandlungsfehlerbegutachtung_Jahresstatistik_2018_PDF_UA.pdf> accessed 15 November 2023

———, *Jahresstatistik 2019. Behandlungsfehler-Begutachtung der MDK-Gemeinschaft* (2020) <https://md-bund.de/fileadmin/dokumente/Pressemitteilungen/2020/2020_06_25/20_06_25_MDK-Behandlungsfehlerbegutachtung_Jahresstatistik_2019_barrierefrei.pdf> accessed 15 November 2023

———, *Behandlungsfehler-Begutachtung der Gemeinschaft der Medizinishen Dienste. Jahresstatistik 2020* (2021) <https://md-bund.de/fileadmin/dokumente/Pressemitteilungen/2021/2021_10_12/4_FIN_-_MD_BEHANDLUNGSFEHLER_BF.pdf> accessed 15 November 2023

———, *Behandlungsfehler-Begutachtung der Gemeinschaft der Medizinischen Dienste Jahresstatistik 2021* (2022) <https://md-bund.de/fileadmin/dokumente/Pressemitteilungen/2022/2022_06_30/22_06_30_PK_BHF_Jahresstatstik_BEHANDLUNGSFEHLER_2021_BF.pdf> accessed 15 November 2022

———, *Behandlungsfehler-Begutachtung der Gemeinschaft der Medizinischen Dienste. Jahresstatistik 2022* (2023) <https://md-bund.de/fileadmin/dokumente/Pressemitteilungen/2023/2023_08_17/PK_BHF_2022_Jahresstatistik.pdf> accessed 15 November 2022

Meurer C, *Außergerichtliche Streitbeilegung in Arzthaftungssache* (Springer 2008)

Michel P et alii, *Étude nationale sur les èvènements indésirables graves liés aux soins* (2006) <https://drees.solidarites-sante.gouv.fr/sites/default/files/2020-10/dtee60.pdf> accessed 13 November 2023

Miller F H, 'Medical Malpractice Litigation: Do the British Have a Better Remedy?' (1986) 11 AJLM 433

Ministero della Giustizia, *Commissione d'Ippolito – Commissione per lo studio e l'approfondimento delle problematiche relative alla colpa professionale medica (28 marzo 2023) – Scheda di sintesi* <www.giustizia.it/giustizia/it/mg_1_36_0.page?contentId=COS424596> accessed 15 September 2023

Ministero della Salute, *Rapporto annuale sull'attività di ricovero ospedaliero. Dati SDO 2008* (2009) <www.salute.gov.it/imgs/C_17_pubblicazioni_1253_allegato.pdf> accessed 16 June 2023

———, *Annuario Statistico del Servizio Sanitario Nazionale. Assetto organizzativo, attività e fattori produttivi del SSN. Anno 2020* (2022) <www.salute.gov.it/imgs/C_17_pubblicazioni_3245_allegato.pdf> accessed 14 September 2023

———, *Commissione consultiva per le problematiche in materia di medicina difensiva e di responsabilita' professionale degli esercenti le professioni sanitarie* <www.quotidianosanita.it/allegati/allegato2684265.pdf> accessed 15 September 2023

Monateri P G, 'Cumulo di azioni', *Digesto delle discipline privatistiche: Sezione civile*, vol 3 (1989)

Moret-Bailly J, 'Assurance, assurance-maladie et État: qui doit payer pour les fautes de médecins?' (2004) Resp civ et assur, alerte 11

Morlet-Haïdara L, Dalle M-C, Riaux I, Jung P et Flavin P, 'Table ronde: focus sur la technique d'assurance' (2023) Resp civ et assur, dossier 24

Moscati E, 'Responsabilità sanitaria e teoria generale delle obbligazioni (note minime sui commi 1 e 3, prima frase, art. 7, l. 8 marzo 2017, n. 24)' (2018) Riv Dir Civ 829

Motta S, Testa D, Cesari U, Quaremba G and Motta G, 'Medical Liability, Defensive Medicine and Professional Insurance in Otolaryngology' (2015) 8 BMC Res Notes 343

Najaf-Zadeha A, Dubosa F, Aurela M, Bons-Letouzeyc C, Amalbertic R and Martinot A, 'Incidence des déclarations de plaintes envers les pédiatres' (2010) 17(2) Archives de pédiatrie 183

Natowicz-Laurent I, 'Les conséquences économiques de l'évolution du droit de la responsabilité civile médicale: un état des lieux' (2007) 117 Revue d'économie politique 963

Neumann G, 'Gutachterkommissionen und Schlichtungsstellen: Eine Evaluation der Ergebnisse' (1998) MedR 309

Nocco L, 'Un no-fault plan come risposta alla "crisi" della responsabilità sanitaria? Uno sguardo sull'"alternativa francese" a dieci anni dalla sua introduzione' (2012) Riv It Med Leg 449

Noguéro S, 'Rapport conclusif. Le risque médical entre solidarité et assurance. 20 ans après la loi About du 30 décembre 2002' (2023) Resp civ et assur, dossier 25

Norelli G-A, De Luca F, Focardi M, Giardiello R and Pinchi V, 'The Claims Management Committees Trial: Experience of an Italian Hospital of the National Health System' (2015) 29 J Forensic Leg Med 6

Observatoire des risques médicaux (ORM), *Rapport d'activité 2015. Années 2009 à 2014* (2015) <www.oniam.fr/medias/uploads/ORM/Rapport_ORM_2015__2009-2014.pdf> accessed 10 November 2023

Office national d'indemnisation des accidents médicaux, des affections iatrogènes et des infections nosocomiales (ONIAM), *Rapport d'activité 2022* (2023) <www.oniam.fr/medias/uploads/RA/ONIAM-RAPPORT_ACTIVITE_2022.pdf> accessed 13 November 2023

Oliphant K and Wright R W (eds), *Medical Malpractice and Compensation in Global Perspective* (De Gruyter 2013)

Olson T and Argent T, 'Responsabilité, assurance et solidarité en matière sanitaire' (2005) AJDA 2226

Osservatorio nazionale delle buone pratiche sulla sicurezza nella sanità, *Indicatori per la sicurezza delle cure. Dicembre 2018* (2018) <www.senato.it/service/PDF/PDFServer/DF/343448.pdf> accessed 21 November 2023

———, *Relazione annuale dicembre 2018* (2018) <www.senato.it/service/PDF/PDFServer/DF/343448.pdf> accessed 21 November 2023

———, *Relazione 2019* (2019) <www.buonepratichesicurezzasanita.it/images/RELAZIONE2019/Relazione_sintetica.pdf> accessed 21 November 2023

———, *Relazione annuale. Dicembre 2021* (2021) <https://documenti.camera.it/_dati/leg18/lavori/documentiparlamentari/IndiceETesti/242/002/INTERO.pdf> accessed 21 November 2023

———, *Relazione annuale. Dicembre 2022* (2022) <www.senato.it/service/PDF/PDFServer/DF/427999.pdf> accessed 21 November 2023

Osservatorio sulla Giustizia Civile di Milano, *Tabelle milanesi per la liquidazione del danno non patrimoniale – Edizione 2021* <www.milanosservatorio.it/wp-content/uploads/2021/03/OSS-MI-TABELLE-2021-LIQUIDAZIONE-DANNO-NON-PATRIMONIALE-ALLA-PERSONA.pdf> accessed 15 September 2023

Osservatorio sulla Responsabilità Medica (OR.Me.), 'Osservatorio Orme: la responsabilità sanitaria, problemi e prospettive' *Sanità24* (23 March 2015) <www.sanita24.ilsole24ore.com/art/commenti/2015-03-23/responsabilita-sanitaria-problemi-prospettive-111614.php?uuid=AbI2JEWL> accessed 8 June 2023

Papeix A-M, 'Contexte et ambitions de la loi About – Le point de vue de l'assureur' (2023) Resp civ et assur, dossier 17

Penneau J, *La responsabilité médicale* (Sirey 1977)

———, 'La réforme de la responsabilité médicale: responsabilité ou assurance' (1990) 42 Rev Intern Dr Comp 525

———, 'Médecine – Médecins', *Répertoire de droit pénal et de procédure pénale*, Octobre 2010 (actualisation: Juin 2022) <www-dalloz-fr> accessed 28 August 2023

Peters T A, *Der strafrechtliche Arzthaftungsprozeß. Eine empirisch-dogmatische Untersuchung in kriminalpolitischer Absicht* (Pro Universitate Verlag 2000)

———, 'Defensivmedizin durch Rechtsunsicherheit im Arztstrafverfahren?' (2003) 21 MedR 219

Petry M, 'Entwicklung der Schadenaufwendungen im Heilwesenrisiko', in Dautert I and Jorzig A (eds), *Arzthaftung – Mängel im Schadensausgleich?* (Springer 2009)
———, 'Haftpflichtschäden in chirurgischen Abteilungen deutscher Krankenhäuser: Zahlen, Ursachen und Konsequenzen' (2010) 43 Gynäkologe 257
———, 'Medical Liability in Germany', in Koch B E (ed), *Medical Liability in Europe: A Comparison of Selected Jurisdictions* (De Gruyter 2011)
———, 'Versicherbarkeit von Krankenhäusern – ein Problemfeld zunehmender Brisanz' (2015) 48 Gynäkologe 621
Pioggia A, *Diritto sanitario e dei servizi sociali* (Giappichelli 2014)
Poli P F, *La colpa grave* (Giuffrè Francis Lefebvre 2021) 77ff
Ponzanelli G, 'La responsabilità medica ad un bivio: assicurazione obbligatoria, sistema residuale no-fault o risk-management?' (2003) Danno e Resp 428
———, 'Medical malpractice: la legge Bianco Gelli' (2017) Contr Impr 356
———, 'Medical malpractice: la legge Bianco Gelli. Una premessa' (2017) Danno e Resp 268
Porchy-Simon S, 'Vingt ans de coexistence de la responsabilité et de la solidarité: bilan prospectif' (2022) Resp civ et assur, dossier 10
Pouletty J and Sarica P, 'La responsabilité civile professionnelle médicale: une approche statistique' (1991) 6 Risques 43 <www.revue-risques.fr/wpcontent/uploads/Risques-006_Web.pdf> accessed 4 July 2023
Preuß J, Dettmeyer R and Madea B, *Begutachtung behaupteter letaler und nicht letaler Behandlungsfehler im Fach Rechtsmedizin. Bundesweite multizentrische Studie im Auftrag des Bundesministeriums für Gesundheit und Soziales (BMGS)* (2005) <www.bundesgesundheitsministerium.de/fileadmin/ Dateien/5_Publikationen/Ministerium/Begutachtung-Behandlungsfehler-Rechtsmedizin.pdf> accessed 14 July 2023
Procaccia C, *Rapport d'information fait au nom de la commission des affaires sociales sur l'assurance responsabilité civile médicale des professionnels de santé libéraux* (2021) <www.senat.fr/rap/r20-693/r20-6931.pdf> accessed 9 November 2023
Püster D, *Entwicklungen der Arzthaftpflichtversicherung* (Springer 2013)
Quadri E, 'Considerazioni in tema di responsabilità medica e di relativa assicurazione nella prospettiva dell'intervento legislativo' (2017) Resp Civ Prev 27
Quézel-Ambrunaz C, 'La réparation des préjudices laissés par les cicatrices. Étude statistique' (2020) D 2248
Radé C, 'La loi Kouchner a 10 ans (déjà)' (2012) Resp civ et assur, alerte 5
Redon M, 'Mesures d'instruction confiées à un technicien (Pr. civ.)', *Répertoire de procédure civile Dalloz* (Mise à jour de novembre 2022) <wwwdalloz-fr> accessed 28 July 2023
Regione Emilia-Romagna, *Report Sinistri del Servizio sanitario della Regione Emilia-Romagna Quadriennio 2008–2011 e aggiornamenti 2012* (2014) <https://assr.regione.emilia-romagna.it/pubblicazioni/rapporti-documenti/ report-sinistri-ssr-2008-2011-2012/@@download/publicationFile/report-sinistri-2008–2012.pdf> accessed 14 June 2023
Regione Emilia-Romagna – Centro per la Gestione del Rischio Sanitario e la Sicurezza del paziente – Osservatorio Regionale per la Sicurezza delle

Cure, *Secondo report regionale sulle fonti informative per la sicurezza delle cure. Anno 2019* <https://salute.regione.emilia-romagna.it/assistenza-ospedaliera/sicurezza-cure/il-sistema-per-la-sicurezza-delle-cure-nella-regione-emilia-romagna/report-2019.pdf> accessed 22 November 2023
———, *Quinto report regionale sulle fonti informative per la sicurezza delle cure. Anno 2022* <https://salute.regione.emilia-romagna.it/assistenza-ospedaliera/sicurezza-cure/le-fonti-informative-per-la-sicurezza-delle-cure/quinto-report-fonti-informative-sicurezza-cure_anno-2022.pdf/@@download/file/Quinto% 20report%20fonti%20informative%20sicurezza%20cure_anno%202022. pdf> accessed 22 November 2023
Regione Lombardia and Aon S.p.A. Insurance & Reinsurance Brokers, *Mappatura del rischio del Sistema Sanitario Regionale. Risultati diciassettesima edizione 31/12/2020* (2021) <www.regione.lombardia.it/wps/wcm/ connect/7bcf1866-49ab-42cf-93de-2f19d67ecf03/XVII+Edizione+Mappa tura+regionale.pdf?MOD=AJPERES&CACHEID=ROOTWORKSPACE-7bcf1866-49ab-42cf-93de-2f19d67ecf03-nQ8.yRB> accessed 13 June 2023
Rehborn M, 'Selbständiges Beweisverfahren im Arzthaftungsrecht?' (1998) (1) MDR 16
Robineau M, 'Le statut normatif de la nomenclature Dintilhac des préjudices' (2010) JCP G, doctr. 612
Romagnoli G, 'Autoassicurazione della responsabilità medica: compatibilità con i principi di diritto interno ed europeo' (2015) Danno e Resp 329
———, 'Limiti di "praticabilità" della c.d. autoassicurazione della responsabilità medica da parte delle amministrazioni sanitarie', in Landini S (ed), *Autoassicurazione e gestione del rischio* (CESIFIN 2015) <www.cesifin.it/ wp-content/uploads/2016/12/AUTOASSICURAZIONE_E_GESTIONE_ DEL_RISCHIO_22_09_15.pdf> accessed 6 October 2023
Ruffolo U, 'Le responsabilità mediche nell'emergenza sanitaria' (2021) Giur It 483
Sacco R, 'Legal Formants: A Dynamic Approach To Comparative Law' (1991) 39 Am J Comp L 1
Sacconi N C, 'Condotta dell'esercente la professione sanitaria e quantificazione del risarcimento' (2018) Resp Civ Prev 1351
Sargos P, 'Réflexions sur les accidents médicaux et la doctrine jurisprudentielle de la Cour de cassation en matière de responsabilité médicale' (1996) D 365
Scarchillo G, 'La responsabilità medica: risarcimento o indennizzo? Riflessioni, evoluzioni e prospettive di diritto comparato' (2017) Resp Civ Prev 1490
Scheppokat K-D and Neu J, 'Der Stellenwert von Schlichtung und Mediation bei Konflikten zwischen Patient und Arzt' (2002) 53 VersR 385
Schlösser G, 'Die Arzthaftpflichtversicherung – Daten, Fakten, Zahlen' (2011) 29 MedR 227
Scognamiglio P, Morena D, Di Fazio N, Delogu G, Iniziato V, La Pia S, Saviano P, Frati P and Fineschi V, '*Vox clamantis in deserto*: A Survey among Italian Psychiatrists on Defensive Medicine and Professional Liability' (2023) 14 Front Psychiatry 1244101
Sebok A J, 'Recovery for Physical Harm: The Case of Medical Malpractice', in Bussani M, Sebok A J and Infantino M (eds), *Common Law and Civil Law Perspectives on Tort Law* (OUP 2022)

Sicot C, 'Responsabilité médicale: l'expérience du groupe des assurances mutuelles médicales (GAMM)' (1998) 182 Bulletin de l'Académie nationale de médecine 541

Singer I, Grotz M, Klotzbach H, Kowalski I, Lemke R, Psathakis D and Skorning M, *Behandlungsfehler-Begutachtung der MDK-Gemeinschaft: Jahresstatistik 2012* (MDS – Medizinischer Dienst des Spitzenverbandes Bund der Krankenkassen e.V., MDK Bayern 2013) <https://md-bund.de/fileadmin/dokumente/Publikationen/GKV/Behandlungsfehler/Bericht_BHF-Begutachtung_2012_final.pdf> accessed 18 July 2023

Singer I, Skorning M and Kowalski I (eds), *Behandlungsfehler-Begutachtung der MDK-Gemeinschaft: Jahresstatistik 2011* (MDS – Medizinischer Dienst des Spitzenverbandes Bund der Krankenkassen e.V., MDK Bayern 2013) <https://md-bund.de/fileadmin/dokumente/Publikationen/GKV/Behandlungsfehler/Bericht_2011_Behandlungsfehler-Begutachtung_MDK-Gemeinschaft.pdf> accessed 18 July 2023

Sloan F A and Chepke L M, *Medical Malpractice* (MIT P 2008)

Soergel P, Schöffski O, Hillemanns P, Hille-Betz U and Kundu S, 'Increasing Liability Premiums in Obstetrics – Analysis, Effects and Options' (2015) 75 Geburtsh Frauenheilk 367

Spickhoff A, 'Die Arzthaftung im neuen bürgerlich-rechtlichen Normenumfeld: Eine erste Zwischenbilanz' (2015) 33 MedR 845

Stafford N, 'German insurers call for central database of complaints against doctors' (2016) 353 BMJ i2815

Statistische Ämter des Bundes und der Länder, *Fachserie. 10, Rechtspflege: Reihe 2, Gerichte und Staatsanwaltschaften.1, Zivilgerichte* <www.statistischebibliothek.de/mir/receive/DESerie_mods_00000101> accessed 27 July 2023

Statistisches Bundesamt, *Rechtspflege Zivilgerichte 2012* (2013) <www.statistischebibliothek.de/mir/servlets/MCRFileNodeServlet/DEHeft_derivate_00012135/2100210127004.pdf> accessed 27 July 2023

———, *Rechtspflege Zivilgerichte 2015* (2016) <www.statistischebibliothek.de/mir/servlets/MCRFileNodeServlet/DEHeft_derivate_00027207/2100210157004.pdf> accessed 15 November 2023

———, *Rechtspflege Zivilgerichte 2021* (2022) <www.statistischebibliothek.de/mir/servlets/MCRFileNodeServlet/DEHeft_derivate_00070926/2100210217004.pdf> accessed 15 November 2023

Stauch M, *The Law of Medical Negligence in England and in Germany: A Comparative Analysis* (Hart 2008)

———, 'Medical Malpractice and Compensation in Germany', in Oliphant K and Wright R W (eds), *Medical Malpractice and Compensation in Global Perspective* (De Gruyter 2013)

———, 'The 2013 German Patients' Rights Act – Codifying Medical Malpractice Compensation' (2015) 6 JETL 85

Tamm M, 'Außergerichtliche Streitbeilegung bei der Arzthaftung: Hat die Mediation neben der Schlichtung eine Chance?' (2017) GesR 764

Tarantino U, Giai Via A, Macrì E, Eramo A, Marino V and Marsella L T, 'Professional Liability in Orthopaedics and Traumatology in Italy' (2013) 471 Clin Orthop Relat Res 3349

Taroni F, *Health and Healthcare Policy in Italy since 1861: A Comparative Approach* (Palgrave Macmillan 2021)

Taroni F and Cicognani A, 'L'istituzionalizzazione del governo del rischio nel servizio sanitario nazionale ed il ruolo della medicina legale' (2007) Riv It Med Leg 1329

Tartaglia R, Albolino S, Bellandi T, Bianchini E, Biggeri A, Fabbro G, Bevilacqua L, Dell'Erba A, Privitera G and Sommella L, 'Eventi avversi e conseguenze prevenibili: studio retrospettivo in cinque grandi ospedali italiani' (2012) 36 Epidemiol Prev 151

Taylor S, 'Providing Redress for Medical Accidents in France: Conflicting Aims, Effective Solutions?' (2011) 2 JETL 57

——, *Medical Accident Liability and Redress in English and French Law* (CUP 2015)

Tercinet M-R, 'Principes généraux de la responsabilité médicale sur le plan administratif' (1998) 28 Méd Mal Infect 41

Terrier E and Penneau J, 'Médecine: réparation des conséquences des risques sanitaires', *Répertoire de droit civil Dalloz* (Octobre 2020, actualisation: Mars 2023) <www-dalloz-fr> accessed 2 May 2023

Tescaro M, 'L'evoluzione del diritto della prescrizione: termini, decorrenze e cause di estensione' (2023) Riv Dir Civ 69

Thouvenin D, *La responsabilité médicale: Analyse des données statistiques disponibles et des arrêts rendus par la Cour de cassation et le Conseil d'Etat de 1984 à 1992* (Flammarion Médicine-Sciences 1995)

Treglia M, Pallocci M, Passalacqua P, Giammatteo J, De Luca L, Mauriello S, Cisterna A M and Marsella L T, 'Medical Liability: Review of a Whole Year of Judgments of the Civil Court of Rome' (2021) 18 Int J Environ Res Public Health 6019, 3–4

Trouiller P, Lopard E, Mantz J and Farman T, 'De la complication médicale à l'indemnisation du préjudice' (2012) 31 Ann Fr Anesth Réanim 626

Trunet P, Le Gall J-R and Lhoste F, 'The Role of Iatrogenic Disease in Admissions to Intensive Care' (1980) 244 JAMA 2617

Vayre P, 'Le risque aléatoire en chirurgie et l'indemnisation de son préjudice en procédure civile' (1998) 123 Chirurgie (Paris) 206

Velliscig L, *Assicurazione e "autoassicurazione" nella gestione dei rischi sanitari. Studio di diritto comparato* (Giuffrè 2018)

Vennedey C, 'Ausgang strafrechtlicher Ermittlungsverfahren gegen Ärzte wegen Verdachts eines Behandlungsfehlers' (PhD thesis, Universität Bonn 2007) <https://bonndoc.ulb.uni-bonn.de/xmlui/bitstream/handle/20.500.11811/2947/1122.pdf?sequence=1> accessed 20 July 2023

Vetrugno G, Foti F, Grassi V M, De-Giorgio F, Cambieri A, Ghisellini R, Clemente F, Marchese L, Sabatelli G, Delogu G, Frati P and Fineschi V, 'Malpractice Claims and Incident Reporting: Two Faces of the Same Coin?' (2022) 19 Int J Environ Res Public Health 16253

Vimercati A, Greco P, Kardashi A, Rossi C, Loizzi V, Scioscia M and Loverro G, 'Choice of Cesarean Section and Perception of Legal Pressure' (2000) 28 J Perinat Med 111

Visintini G, *Trattato breve della responsabilità civile* (Cedam 2005)

Wagner G, 'BGB § 630h', Rn. 1–3, in Säcker F J, Rixecker R, Oetker H and Limperg B (eds), *Münchener Kommentar zum Bürgerlichen Gesetzbuch* (9th edn, Beck 2023)

Weber M, *Economy and Society: An Outline of Interpretive*, vol 2 (Roth G and Wittich C eds, UC Press, 1978)

Weidinger P, 'Gutachterkommissionen und Schlichtungsstellen aus Sicht eines Arzthaftpflichtversicherers' (2003) VW 674

———, 'Aus der Praxis eines Heilwesenversicherers: Aktuelle Entwicklungen in der Arzt- und Krankenhaushaftpflicht' (2004) 22 MedR 289

———, 'Aus der Praxis der Haftpflichtversicherung für Ärzte und Krankenhäuser – Statistik, neue Risiken und Qualitätsmanagement' (2006) 24 MedR 571

Weiler P C, *Medical Malpractice on Trial* (HUP 1991)

Weltrich H, Beck L and Smentkowski U, 'Erfolgreiche Streitschlichtung. Neue Evaluation der Gutachterkommission für ärztliche Behandlungsfehler bei der Ärztekammer Nordrhein – Hohe Quote außergerichtlicher Erledigungen' (1998) (5) Rh ÄBl 10

Wheat K, 'Is There a Medical Malpractice Crisis in the UK?' (2005) J Law Med Ethics 444

Woolf H, *Accessto Justice: To the Lord Chancellor on the Civil Justice System in England and Wales* (H.M. Stationery Office 1996)

Zaed I, Menna G, Auricchio A M, Servadei F, Garbossa D, Olivi A and Della Pepa G M, 'Medicolegal Issues: Perception, Awareness, and Behavioral Changes Among Italian Neurosurgical Community: Survey-Based Analysis' (2021) 154 World Neurosurg e774

Zimmermann R, *Comparative Foundations of a European Law of Set-Off and Prescription* (CUP 2002)

Index

114   *Index*

Istituto per la vigilanza sulle assicurazioni (IVASS) 36, 80

legal formants 5
legge Gelli-Bianco 60–4, 66–7, 79–81, 86–7, 88–9, 93–4
limitation periods *see* statute of limitations
loi About 54
loi Kouchner 50–4, 68, 71, 87, 93–4
long-stop 10, 12, 53–4, 66, 88–9, 93

Mac Aleese commission 49
Medizinische Dienst der Krankenversicherung (MDK) 31–2, 47, 78–9, 88, 90, 94

no-fault compensation scheme 49, 51, 55, 71, 92, 94

obbligazione di mezzi 12–13
obligations de moyens 7, 10
Observatoire des risques médicaux (ORM) 73–4
Office national d'indemnisation des accidents médicaux, des affections iatrogènes et des infections nosocomiales (ONIAM) 52, 54, 73–4, 75–6; *référentiel* 76

Patientenrechtegesetz 55–7, 65, 77, 92
premiums 4, 25–7, 37–8, 47, 86, 89; experience rated 45; set by the *bureau central de tarification* 54; after the reforms 68–70, 77, 80–1
pre-trial orders 14–15, 60, 64, 67, 74, 82

reinsurance 4
risk retention *see* self-retention
Robert Koch Institut 24

Schlichtungsstellen 27–30, 47, 67, 77–8, 88, 93–4
Schuldrechtsmodernisierungsgesetz 55, 66, 93
self-retention 66–7, 88–90, 93; in France 19; in Germany 26; in Italy 35, 38, 47, 54, 62–4, 81
statute of limitations 66, 88–9, 92–3, 95; in France 6–7, 51, 53–4, 75; in Germany 9–10, 55–6; Italy 12, 38–9, 61–2, 63, 80, 85
strict liability 8, 13, 51, 66, 92

Zweites Schadensersatzrechtsänderungsgesetz 55

For Product Safety Concerns and Information please contact our EU
representative GPSR@taylorandfrancis.com
Taylor & Francis Verlag GmbH, Kaufingerstraße 24, 80331 München, Germany